The Lord's Presence

Alton H. McEachern

D1118481

BROADMAN PRESS
Nashville, Tennessee

To
Doctor Michael G. Queen
Colleague in Ministry
Fellow Servant of The Word

Library of Congress Cataloging-in-Publication Data

McEachern, Alton H.
  The Lord's presence.

  Includes bibliographical references.
  1. Lord's Supper—Sermons. 2. Jesus Christ—
Presence—Sermons. 3. Sermons, American. 4. Baptists—
Sermons. 5. Lord's Supper—Liturgy—Texts. I. Title.
BV4257.5.M29 1986   234′.163   85-17172
ISBN 0-8054-2314-1

Acknowledgments

I want to express my appreciation to the deacons and congregation of the First Baptist Church of Greensboro. Their encouragement of this extended ministry of writing has been a joy; they have made it possible for me to write during the past twelve years.

I am indebted to my associate, Michael G. Queen. His dedicated work and loyalty have helped me care for the people of God—and to write.

This volume is enriched by orders of worship prepared by Minister of Music Douglas Peoples and his music assistant, Mrs. Ray Anderson.

The task of expert typing has been performed by secretary to the pastor, Mrs. Shelba Forrest, assisted by Mrs. Dot Holleman and Mrs. Lynn Rumley.

The Lord's Supper devotionals included in this volume have been prepared and delivered across the past eight years at the First Baptist Church of Greensboro.

A. H. Mc.

Preface

One autumn I studied at the College of Preachers in Washington, D. C. I asked my roommate, "What does the Lord's Supper mean to you?" He replied in three words, "The real Presence." My new friend may have meant more by that phrase than I would buy as a Baptist. However, it set me thinking.

We believe that God is present in His world in many ways. Surely He is present in nature. The creation reflects and reminds us of its Creator. "In the rustling grass I hear him pass,/He speaks to me ev'rywhere."[1]

God is present in and speaks through history for those who see and hear. He is certainly present in the human conscience. This is called general revelation. Special revelation refers to the fact that God speaks to us through the Scriptures and in the person of His Son, Jesus Christ, the Living Word. We experience God's focused presence in our worship at the Lord's table.

Look at the Supper's Significance

The observance of the Lord's Supper begins with *a backward look.* Jesus said, "Do this in remembrance of me" (Luke 22:19).

In AD 53, a scant thirty years after the crucifixion, Paul wrote our earliest account of the institution of the Lord's Supper. It was already being handed down as an oral tradition in the churches. Note the formula of the loaf and cup in 1 Corinthians 11:23-25:

Jesus took bread saying, "This is my body which is for you. Do this in remembrance of me."

The Master took the cup from the passover table saying, "This cup is the new covenant in my blood . . . drink it, in remembrance of me" (v. 25).

Just as the old covenant was sealed with blood and a meal eaten "before the Lord," so the new covenant is recalled by a memorial meal. "For Christ, our paschal lamb, has been sacrificed" (1 Cor. 5:7). The Lord's Supper calls us to look at the cross.

Our observance also calls for *an inward look* (1 Cor. 11:27-29). It is possible to be guilty of irreverence toward the body and blood of the Lord. Thus, we have a call to self-examination before we take the elements—eat the bread and drink the cup. This is a time for spiritual inventory. We look to our relationship with God and other persons.

The Lord's Supper calls for *a forward look* as well (1 Cor. 11:26): "For as often as you eat this bread and drink the cup, you proclaim the Lord's death until he comes." The observance has a future reference. It is eschatological. We look forward to Christ's return in glory.

> Paschal Lamb, by God appointed,
>   all our sins on Thee were laid:
> By almighty love anointed,
>   Thou hast full atonement made.
> All Thy people are forgiven,
>   through the virtue of Thy blood;
> Opened in the gate of heaven;
>   peace is made "twixt man and God."[2]

In our worship at the Lord's table, we take *an outward look* (1 Cor. 11:26). "You proclaim the Lord's death." The supper is an enacted Word. By participation in it we herald—announce—our faith.

We look outward from the worship service to the world's need: people are lost, hungry, weary, and in pain. The observance is a call to Christian service.

• The Lord's Supper calls us to remember and proclaim Christ's sacrificial death.

• It invites us to celebrate His living Presence in our midst.

• It fixes our hope on the final victory to be realized at His coming.

> Draw thou my soul, O Christ, Closer to thine;
> Breathe into ev'ry wish Thy will divine!
> Raise my low self above, Won by thy deathless love;
> Ever, O Christ, thro' mine Let thy life shine.

Lead forth my soul, O Christ, One with thine own,
Joyful to follow thee Thro' paths unknown!
In thee my strength renew; Give me my work to do!
Thro' me thy truth be shown, Thy love made known.

Not for myself alone May my prayer be;
Lift thou thy world, O Christ, Closer to thee!
Cleanse it from guilt and wrong; Teach it salvation's song,
Till earth, as heav'n, fulfill God's holy will.[3]

This book combines orders of worship and Lord's Supper devotionals for use by worship leaders. It is a sequel to a book published earlier by Broadman Press, *Here at Thy Table, Lord.* I hope that the use of these materials will enrich your worship at the Lord's Table as they have for us at the First Baptist Church of Greensboro, North Carolina.

From *The White Columns*
ALTON HOWARD MCEACHERN

Contents

1
Realize Christ's Presence

SACRED ORGAN MUSIC
        "My Heart Is Filled with Longing" Bach-Schreiner
CALL TO WORSHIP   "All Glory Be to God on High"   Lunquist
INVOCATION
HYMN   "Holy, Holy, Holy"   Dykes
                          Organ Meditation
WORDS OF WELCOME
HYMN   "We Believe in One True God"
    (Hymn: "For the Beauty of the Earth; Tune: DIX)
CALL TO PRAYER   PASTORAL PRAYER
THE MORNING OFFERING
Anthem   "Gloria in Excelsis"   Mozart
Gloria Patri
Responsive Reading

> *Leader:* In the name of Christ our Lord we have gathered as one people to worship the One True God.
>
> *People:* Give us a keen awareness of Your presence, O God.
>
> *Leader:* We have come to offer our praise, confess our sins, give of our means, and commit ourselves to Christlike service.
>
> *People:* Give us a clear vision of who we are and what Your eternal purpose is, O God.
>
> *Leader:* We come with open minds and receptive hearts to be responsive to God's Word and leadership.
>
> *People:* Give us the courage to respond with joy, O God![4]

SERMON   "Lord's Supper—Realize Christ's Presence"

In Matthew 18:20 we have a magnificent promise from Jesus: "Where two or three come together in my name, I am there with them" (GNB).

Christ promises to be in our midst. He is in our corporate worship, prayer, and observance of the Lord's Supper. This text is not a consolation for a poor turnout. The term *two or three* is an idiom for a group of any size, large or small. The important truth in this verse is not the size of the crowd but the Presence of the Christ.

We can be sure this promise from the Master was a comfort to the first century church. They were a tiny island of believers in a sea of paganism. Christ is present in our prayer meetings and Bible study groups as surely as He is present in the church sanctuary or coliseum crusade.

This lovely text reminds us that Christ is present in our family worship. "Where two [a man and his wife] or three [along with their child] come together in my name, I am there with them." Christ is Lord of the dinner table in our homes as surely as he is Lord of the communion table at church.

Remember that "little is much when God is in it." God opened the Wall of China to diplomatic relations with a Ping-Pong ball. Many times He accomplishes great purposes with small means.

Christ is present in our private prayer and public worship. Once, in Russia, a government agent attended a worship service and took down the names of all in attendance. One worshiper said to him, "There is one Person present whose name you do not have."

"No," protested the soviet agent. "I have the name of everyone here."

"Jesus Christ is here!" said the believer.

God is *universally* present in the world. Psalm 19:1 sings, "The heavens declare the glory of God; and the firmament sheweth his handiwork" (KJV). There is no place in creation where God is not present. I served on an ordination council for a man who had tried to escape the call of God to ministry. He had joined the navy but found that the Almighty was on the other side of the world as well as at home.

God's presence in the world is inescapable. Listen to the compelling poetry of Psalm 139:7-12:

> Whither shall I go from thy Spirit?
> Or whither shall I flee from thy presence?
> If I ascend to heaven, thou art there!
> If I make my bed in Sheol, thou art there!
> If I take the wings of the morning and dwell in the
> uttermost parts of the sea,
> even there thy hand shall lead me,
> and thy right hand shall hold me.
> If I say, "Let only darkness cover me,
> and the light about me be night,"
> even the darkness is not dark to thee,
> the night is bright as the day;
> for darkness is as light with thee.

This passage inspired poet Francis Thompson to write about "The Hound of Heaven."

God is *particularly* present in His world. At specific times and places His Presence has been obvious and transforming. In Old Testament times, God called Moses at the burning bush. He called Abraham to leave his homeland and go on a pilgrimage of faith—he knew not where. God was present in the Temple worship and called young Isaiah to be His prophet. God was also present in great events, such as the Exodus and the Israelite's return from Exile.

In New Testament times, the divine Presence was not in doubt. "In Christ God was reconciling the world to himself" (2 Cor. 5:19). Jesus was God incarnate—"The Word became flesh and dwelt among us" (John 1:14).

God is particularly present today in our worship: prayer and praise, the preaching of the Word, the drama of baptism, and the Lord's Supper.

If you will be confessional, you may acknowledge that God has been present in your life. It may have been in a time of danger when you cried, "O God! Help me!" and he did. I recall experiencing such a moment while driving across an ice-covered bridge in north Georgia and losing control of the car.

God may have been present in your experience at some point of temptation. You asked for His help, and He provided a way out.

The divine Presence may well have been yours in a time of trouble or grief. In the midst of great loss or disappointment, you felt comfort as you sensed His Presence with you.

God can be with us in our daily walk. We learn to practice the Presence of the Lord. Begin your prayer times by acknowledging that He is with you. "He walks with me, and he talks with me,/And he tells me I am his own."

Is Christ real in your experience? Are you consciously aware of the divine Presence? Luther declared, "God is here." He also expressed an even more significant thought: "God is here *for you.*" Can you acknowledge that and rejoice in it? None are so blind as those who refuse to see.

The observance of the Lord's Supper invites us into God's Presence to worship and have fellowship with Him. Jesus said, "Do this in remembrance of me" (Luke 22:19). The observance then sends us back to our responsibilities in the world with new freedom and joy. It constitutes a call to worship and a call to serve. In the Lord's Supper, we experience the Presence of Christ cognito—in fact.

As we come to the table,

> may Christ enter our minds, that we may think his thoughts;
> may Christ flood our emotions, that we may feel his love;
> may Christ captivate our wills, that we may follow where he leads;
> may Christ fill our bodies, to heal and to bless.

> O Love that wilt not let me go,
> I rest my weary soul in thee;
> I give thee back the life I owe,
> That in thine ocean depths its flow
> May richer, fuller be.
>   —*George Matheson*

OBSERVANCE OF THE LORD'S SUPPER

Giving of the Bread
   Soloist   "As We Gather Around the Table" Blankenship
Giving of the Cup
   Anthem   "Agnus Dei" from "Misa Dixit Maria"   Hassler
                     Ensemble
   "Lamb of God, Thou that takest away the sins of the world
   O have mercy on us."
HYMN   "When I Survey the Wondrous Cross"   Mason
SHARING OF DECISIONS
BENEDICTION   MOMENT OF SILENCE   ORGAN DISMISSAL

2
Inescapable

PRELUDE   Sacred Organ Music
HYMN   "Majestic Sweetness Sits Enthroned"   Hastings
HYMN   "What a Friend We Have in Jesus"   Converse
WELCOME AND PRAYER
THE EVENING OFFERING
   OFFERTORY   "He Watching Over Israel"   Mendelssohn
   Offertory Prayer
HYMN   "There's a Wideness in God's Mercy"   Tourjee
SOLO   (based on Psalm 77)   Fettke
SERMON   "The Lord's Presence—Inescapable"

"They heard the sound of the Lord God walking in the garden in the cool of the day, and the man and his wife hid themselves from the presence of the Lord God among the trees of the garden. But the Lord God called to the man, and said to him, "Where are you?" (Gen. 3:8-9).

Whither shall I go from thy Spirit?/Or whither shall I flee from thy presence?/If I ascend to heaven, thou art there!/If I make my bed in Sheol, thou art there!/If I take the wings of the morning/and dwell in the uttermost parts of the sea,/even there thy hand shall lead me,/and thy right hand shall hold me./If I say, "Let only darkness cover me,/and the light about me be night,"/even the darkness is not dark to thee,/the night is bright as the day;/for darkness is as light with thee (Ps. 139:7-12).

God could have abandoned Adam and Eve in the garden of Eden after the fall. He could have given up on them due to their sin. But He came seeking, searching, asking, "Adam, where are you?" This was not a question of location. It was a question of divine love. God knew where Adam was physically. What God wanted was to lead Adam to take responsibility for his actions.

Jesus said of Himself, "For the Son of man came to seek and to save the lost" (Luke 19:10). In Luke 15 we have three of Jesus' parables: the lost sheep, the lost coin, and the lost boys. Each of these memorable stories depicts God as One who seeks the lost.

The Lord's presence is inescapable. In the biblical story of Jonah, we find a nationalistic prophet. Jonah was a superpatriot who resented God's universal love of all nations. When the Lord called him to prophesy in Nineveh, he did not want to—not for fear of failure. He was afraid he might succeed. If he preached and they repented, God would forgive and spare the people of Nineveh. Jonah preferred to see them blasted!

In an effort to escape the call of God to go and preach in Nineveh, Jonah took a ship to Spain at the far end of the Mediterranean world. As we all know, his escape was rudely intercepted by a great fish!

In this experience, Jonah learned that God cares for all people and nations—not simply our own. There was also the gospel of a second chance in Jonah's experience. When he repented and prayed, he was forgiven and given another opportunity. He eventually went to Nineveh, preached, and saw his message received. The greatest lesson for Jonah was that the Lord's presence is inescapable.

Now consider the message found in Psalm 139. The divine Presence is real in heaven, on earth, and even in Sheol (the grave or the abode of the dead). The poet sang, "If I take the wings of the morning"—go with the sunrise. Flying from the United States to Europe one spends the shortest night of one's life. One is going toward the sunrise. Day breaks about 2:00 AM, New York time.

The psalmist also sang, "If I . . . dwell in the uttermost parts of the sea,/even there . . . thy right hand shall hold me." I served as a member of an ordination council. The minister being examined gave his testimony to the examining group. He had felt the call of God to the ministry when a young man. But he was not interested in preaching. Instead, he joined the U. S. Navy. However, this did not enable him to escape the call. To his amazement, the divine Presence was equally as strong on the far side of the earth, and the sense of call was as insistent as ever. Finally, he gave in to it and became a minister.

The poet concluded that even the darkness is not dark to God. We may go through dark days of doubt, failure, guilt, or grief. But the Heavenly Father is always with us. We can count on His presence and help.

The Lord's presence is inescapable. Saul tried to evade it and kicked "against the pricks" (Acts 9:5, KJV). However, he eventually had to confront the Lord and faith's claim. He became the missionary apostle Paul.

Francis Thompson ran from the Lord and His calling. He was a religious man who grew up in a Christian home. He studied for the Christian ministry. Giving up on that, he studied for medicine. And failing at that, he became a drug addict. Francis Thompson came to the point where he had absolutely nothing left except his love of poetry. A publisher found him in a pathetic and bereft condition, a ragged beggar with no shirt on his back and bare feet. The publisher rescued Francis Thompson, who then began to write. This time he wrote his most famous poem, "The Hound of Heaven."

> I fled Him, down the nights and down the days;
>   I fled Him, down the arches of the years;
> I fled Him, down the labyrinthine ways
>   Of my own mind; and in the midst of tears

I hid from Him, and under running laughter.
    Up vistaed hopes I sped;
    And shot, precipitated,
Adown Titanic glooms of chasméd fears.
  From those strong Feet that followed, followed after.
    But with unhurrying chase,
    And unperturbéd pace,
  Deliberate speed, majestic instancy,
    They beat—and a Voice beat
    More instant than the Feet—
  "All things betray thee, who betrayest Me."[5]

Francis Thompson learned that the Lord's presence is inescapable. He pursues us, not simply to hound us but to help us. He pursues not like some special agent or bounty hunter. He pursues us in love, calling us to faith and to follow.

The Lord's presence is inescapable. Adam and Eve learned it in the garden. Jonah learned it in the belly of a great fish. The psalmist learned it in his despair. Francis Thompson learned it when he fell so low he had to reach up to touch bottom, and we may learn it at the Lord's table. The Lord's presence is inescapable. He is here. His presence is symbolized by broken bread and poured-out fruit of the vine. This observance calls us to remember that we never escape the divine Presence. In fact, we come now to meet Him at the Lord's table.

OBSERVANCE OF THE LORD'S SUPPER
  PASSING OF THE BREAD
    Instrumental Meditation   "Pass Me Not, O Gentle Savior"
                                                Crosby
  PASSING OF THE CUP
    Instrumental Meditation "Nearer My God, To Thee" Adams
HYMN   "Blest Be the Tie"   Mason

3
And Absence

SACRED ORGAN MUSIC   "Sanctus"   Guonod
CALL TO WORSHIP
HYMN   "Holy, Holy, Holy"   Dukes
SCRIPTURE READING   Job 23
HYMN   "Be Thou My Vision"
               Announcements
WORDS OF WELCOME

                         Pastoral Prayer
CALL TO PRAYER
MORNING OFFERING AND FELLOWSHIP OFFERING
   ANTHEM   "The Prayers I Make"   Marshall
                Choir
   GLORIA PATRI
   PRAYER OF DEDICATION

SERMON   "The Lord's Presence—and Seeming Absence"

> Then Job answered:
> "Today also my complaint is bitter,
> his hand is heavy in spite of my groaning.
> Oh, that I knew where I might find him,
>   that I might come even to his seat!
> I would lay my case before him
>   and fill my mouth with arguments.
> I would learn what he would answer me,
>   and understand what he would say to me.
> Would he contend with me in the

17

greatness of his power?
No; he would give heed to me.
There an upright man could reason with him,
and I should be acquitted for ever
by my judge.

"Behold, I go forward, but he is not there;
and backward, but I cannot perceive him;
on the left hand I seek him, but I
cannot behold him;
I turn to the right hand, but I
cannot see him.
But he knows the way that I take;
when he has tried me, I shall come
forth as gold" (Job 23:1-10).

In Shakespeare's play, *Hamlet,* Hamlet's uncle killed his father, the king of Denmark, and married his mother, the queen. Hamlet was bent on avenging this crime. One day he came upon his uncle, the guilt-ridden king, alone—at his prayers. However, Hamlet refused to take advantage of the situation and kill his uncle. Hamlet was afraid that if he killed him while he was praying, the uncle might go to heaven. That was not the destination Hamlet had in mind for his father's murderer.

The king complained privately, "My words fly up, my thoughts remain below:/Words without thoughts never to heaven go."

There are times when the heavens appear to be brass to us. Our prayers cannot seem to get through. This experience is called, in the words of St. John of the Cross "The Dark Night of the Soul." God's absence is experienced by saintly people at times.

The Seeming Absence of God

At times our prayer requests are denied. This may be because what we ask is not really best for us. Or it may not be in God's will for us. Or the timing may be off, and God must answer, "Not yet" or "Not now." When our petitions are not granted, the Father may have something far better in store for us. A friend once remarked, "God does not give us what we ask. He gives better than we ask."

Job felt abandoned by God. He cried out, "Oh, that I knew where I might find him!" These are "my autumn days," he moaned. Job's anguish was real. He cried out at the silence of God, but the Almighty refused to answer his pleas for relief from his suffering. Job felt he had been abandoned by God—*absconditus.* The Lord appeared to be far away.

Faith's greatest test comes when our prayers go unanswered. All our requests appear to be met with stony silence. This can be an awful experience, indeed.

• Moses prayed to enter the Promised Land. It was the goal of his life. Reaching the Promised Land was the obsession of his forty-year ministry, yet it was not to be. He died on Mount Nebo, within sight of the land.

• Paul "besought the Lord" three times that his thorn in the flesh might be removed (2 Cor. 12:8). It was an impediment to his mission work, but the apostle's earnest request was denied. He was assured that God's grace was sufficient for him.

• Jesus prayed repeatedly in Gethsemane that "the cup" might pass without His having to drink it. No one wants to die at thirty-three. Jesus shrank from suffering and death on the cross. Still He prayed, "Nevertheless not my will, but thine, be done" (Luke 22:42).

Why do we on occasion seem to experience the absence of God? Why are our prayers not always answered? At times we pray incorrectly—in the wrong spirit or not in accordance with God's will. We may pray from a sinful heart. There are unrepented sins or dark resentments in our lives. We may pray selfishly. There are times when we are stubborn or arrogantly insist on our will being done.

We may experience the absence of God because we look for Him in the wrong way. Martin Luther sought the Lord for years, but He was trying to earn His salvation. Only when Martin saw salvation as being by grace alone did God find Martin. The silence or seeming absence of God is a dreadful experience.

The Lord's Supper Celebrates the Presence of God

"Then you will call upon me and come and pray to me, and I will hear you. You will seek me and find me; when you seek me with all

your heart, I will be found by you, says the Lord" (Jer. 29:12-14).
Clyde T. Francisco called this the most beautiful passage in Scripture.
Remember that the prophet Elijah realized God's presence not in the
storm, earthquake, or fire. God became real to him in a "still, small
voice" (1 Kings 19:12). Jesus reminded us to "Ask, and it will be given
you; seek, and you will find; knock, and it will be opened to you"
(Matt. 7:7).

Jesus taught that God seeks us. This is one of the lofty insights of
Scripture. In one passage, Luke 15, the Master told three parables
about a lost sheep, a lost coin, and lost sons. All three stories depict
God as One who seeks those who are lost. If Plato taught that God
is found through reason and Buddha taught that we find God in
contemplation, the Bible teaches that God discloses Himself. He finds
us.

The Lord's Supper is an opportunity to realize God's presence
through worship. The supper is characterized by powerful symbols.
They are reminders of the high cost of our salvation—Christ's body
and life's blood given on our behalf. The risen Christ is present with
us in our worship. He promised that whenever we gather in His name,
He is in our midst.

As we wait to receive the broken bread, let us confess our sins to
God. Then, as we wait to receive the fruit of the vine, let us thank God
for the assurance of His pardon. We can appropriate divine forgive-
ness by repentance and faith. "Your sins are forgiven," Jesus said
(Matt. 9:2). "Go, and do not continue in sin" (see John 5:14; 8:11,
AT).

When we encounter God, He turns our question marks into excla-
mation marks of praise. He can make the crooked straight. Job exult-
ed, "When he has tried me, I shall come forth as gold" (v. 10).

The absence of God can be real—and so can His presence, here at
His table.

OBSERVANCE OF THE LORD'S SUPPER

   Giving of the Bread

      Instrumental Meditation   "No, Not Despairingly"   Kerrick

           No, not despairingly Come I to thee,
           No, not distrustingly bend I the knee:

Sin hath gone over me, Yet this is still my plea:
Jesus hath died.
Faithful and just art thou, Forgiving all;
Loving and kind art thou When poor ones call:
Lord, let the cleansing blood, Blood of the Lamb of God,
Pass o'er my soul.

Giving of the Cup

Anthem	"None Other Lamb"	Marshall
	Choir	
HYMN	"Draw Thou My Soul, O Christ"	Sullivan
SHARING OF DECISIONS		Benediction
MOMENT OF SILENCE		Organ Dismissal

4
In Our Consciences

SACRED ORGAN MUSIC "My Heart is Filled with Longing" Bach
CALL TO WORSHIP
HYMN OF ADORATION "Great Redeemer, We Adore Thee" Conte
WORDS OF WELCOME
Guests are invited to meet the pastor and his wife in the church
parlor following morning worship.
HYMN OF THE CHRISTIAN LIFE
"Strong, Righteous Man of Galilee"   Dykes
SCRIPTURE READING
CALL TO PRAYER   Pastoral Prayer
THE MORNING OFFERING
ANTHEM   "The Morning Star"   Sjolund
Congregational Response   Stuttgart
Grant us, Lord, the grace of giving
With a spirit large and free

That ourselves and all our living
We may offer unto Thee. Amen.
    Prayer of Dedication

SERMON   "The Lord's Presence—In Our Consciences"

"The heart is deceitful above all things and desperately corrupt; who can understand it?" (Jer. 17:9).

"He showed me: behold, the Lord was standing beside a wall built with a plumb line, with a plumb line in his hand. And the Lord said to me, 'Amos, what do you see?' And I said, 'A plumb line.' Then the Lord said, 'Behold, I am setting a plumb line in the midst of my people Israel; I will never again pass by them.' " (Amos 7:7-8).

"For I received from the Lord what I also delivered to you, that the Lord Jesus on the night when he was betrayed took bread, and when he had given thanks, he broke it, and said, 'This is my body which is for you. Do this in remembrance of me.' In the same way also the cup, after supper, saying, 'This cup is the new covenant in my blood. Do this, as often as you drink it, in remembrance of me.' For as often as you eat this bread and drink the cup, you proclaim the Lord's death until he comes.

"Whoever, therefore, eats the bread or drinks the cup of the Lord in an unworthy manner will be guilty of profaning the body and blood of the Lord. Let a man examine himself, and so eat of the bread and drink of the cup." (1 Cor. 11:23-28).

God the Creator has not left Himself without a witness in the earth. Nature bears witness to the Lord, "The heavens declare the glory of God" (Ps. 19:1, KJV). The prophets spoke as God directed. "The word of the Lord came to" Jeremiah, Isaiah, Amos, Hosea, and others. The Holy Scriptures bear a powerful witness to God. They are inspired (literally "God-breathed") and are profitable to us. God's supreme self-revelation was in the person of His Son.

God is present and speaks as well through the human conscience—the "still, small voice," that inner sense of ought. The problem is that one's conscience can be devastating, creating an enormous sense of guilt. The conscience can lead us to God or to despair. Huckleberry Finn quipped to the effect that the conscience "takes up more room than all the rest of a person's insides."

Conscience can be bad (Jer. 17:9). "The heart [or conscience] is deceitful above all things,/and desperately corrupt" (wicked, KJV). This text literally states that "the heart is a Jacob"—a deceiver and trickster.

The conscience can be confusing. It is often conditioned by our culture more than informed by Scripture. Conscience can make you think something is wrong when it is right. Or it can make you think something is right when it is wrong (such as racial prejudice).

One's conscience can also play dead—"play possum"—refusing to function. At times the human conscience can be highly destructive. Guilt may tick away like an internal time bomb which can blow your life apart.

Conscience can also be good (Amos 7:7-8). One's conscience can prove to be constructive—like the hearth that holds hot coals, preventing them from burning the house down. Conscience can be our standard of straightness, our plumb line. The church should be the conscience of society, teaching and exemplifying moral values.

Conscience can be the Voice of God. It is that inner sense of ought which shows us what is right and wrong. The gospel teaches that God loves us as we are. That is grace. Conscience then should be like the beams of the cross: vertical, reaching out to our fellow beings.

Some have contended that the conscience is a strange affair. It needs periodic correction. Still, it points toward magnetic moral north—and God.

"Let a man examine himself, and so eat of the bread and drink of the cup" (1 Cor. 11:28).

After this self-examination, we may come to the Lord's table with assurance of divine pardon.

OBSERVANCE OF THE LORD'S SUPPER
  Giving of the Bread
    Solo   "When I Survey the Wondrous Cross" Arr. Harris
  Giving of the Cup
    Chorale   "All for Jesus"   Stainer
                            Choir
HYMN   "Jesus, Keep Me Near the Cross"   Doane
SHARING OF DECISIONS   Benediction
MOMENT OF SILENCE   Organ Dismissal

5
In Others

PRELUDE   "Fountainhead"   Allured
                    Handbell Choir

OPENING PRAYER
HYMN OF ADORATION   "All Hail the Power of Jesus' Name"
                                              Shrubsole

WORDS OF WELCOME
HYMN OF THE CHURCH "The Church's One Foundation" Wesley
SCRIPTURE READING   Call to Prayer   Pastoral Prayer
THE MORNING OFFERING AND FELLOWSHIP OFFERING
  Anthem   Titus 2:11-14   Price
                            Choir

  Congregational Response
            All things are Thine: no gift have we,
            Lord of all gifts, to offer Thee;
            And hence with grateful hearts today,
            Thine own before Thy feet we lay. Amen.
  Prayer of Dedication

SERMON   "The Lord's Presence—In Others"

"Then God said, 'Let us make man in our image, after our likeness; and let them have dominion over the fish of the sea, and over the birds of the air, and over the cattle, and over all the earth, and over every creeping thing that creeps upon the earth.'

"So God created man in his own image, in the image of God he created him; male and female he created them. And God blessed them, and God said to them, 'Be fruitful and multiply, and fill the earth and subdue it; and have dominion over the fish of the sea and over the birds of the air and over every living thing that moves upon the earth.'

"And God said, 'Behold, I have given you every plant yielding seed which is upon the face of all the earth, and every tree with seed in its fruit; you shall have them for food.

" 'And to every beast of the earth, and to every bird of the air, and to everything that creeps on the earth, everything that has the breath of life, I have given every green plant for food.' And it was so. And God saw everything that he had made, and behold, it was very good. And there was evening and there was morning, a sixth day" (Gen. 1:26-31).

God is present in other people. He is not present in the lives of saints alone but in all kinds of people:

• Brilliant and educated people like the apostle Paul, John Calvin, and E. Y. Mullins,

• Uneducated people like William Carey, the cobbler, and William Booth, the pawnbroker's assistant,

• Famous people like Billy Graham and obscure people like the unknown preacher whose sermon touched the heart of Charles Haddon Spurgeon.

James Carter contends that God uses all kinds of people. The only requirement is their willingness to be used.

I spoke to the Rotary Club in Kannapolis, North Carolina. The retired superintendent of schools told me this story. There was a preacher at one of the Baptist churches "who couldn't preach a lick," but he dearly loved people. The preacher brought an eighth grade dropout to the educator. He arranged a two-year course for the young man to graduate. The youth went on to college and seminary, receiving a doctor of philosophy degree. He later taught Christian ethics at Stetson University and the Southern Baptist Theological Seminary. His name: Henlee H. Barnette. God uses all sorts of people. Boris Pasternak reminded us that in the kingdom of God there are only persons.

We believe the Lord is in people because human beings were made in the *image of God*. This means we have freedom of choice, and we have the capacity to know our Maker.

The *incarnation* is further proof that God is present in people. "In Christ God was reconciling the world to himself" (2 Cor. 5:19). God was uniquely present, enfleshed in Jesus.

The *indwelling* of God in believers also speaks of the divine Presence. "Christ in you, the hope of glory" (Col. 1:27).

Jesus' priority was people. He placed them above institutions— even religious institutions such as the Temple and sabbath observance. He was always willing to take time with people. Jesus put people first.

Ours is a corporate faith, not simply an individual one. We are members of the family of God and "priests" to each other. Recall who led you to Christ, who baptized you, taught and encouraged you, prayed for you.

Yes, God is present—in others.

> People who know go to people who need to know Jesus;
> People who love go to people alone without Jesus;
> For there are people who need to see,
>   people who need to love,
>   people who need to know God's redeeming love.
> People who see go to those who are blind without Jesus,
> And this is people to people, yes,
>   people to people,
> All sharing together God's love.[6]

OBSERVANCE OF THE LORD'S SUPPER

Giving of the Bread		
Solo	"O Lord Most Holy"	Franck
Giving of the Cup		
Meditation	"The Lord's Supper"	Van Hemert
	Handbell Choir	
HYMN OF INVITATION	"Blest Be the Tie"	Mason
SHARING OF DECISIONS		BENEDICTION
MOMENT OF SILENCE		ORGAN DISMISSAL

6
In Heaven

PRELUDE	"Procession"	Hopson
	"Joyful Praise"	Hopson
	Handbell Choir	
CALL TO WORSHIP		
HYMN OF PRAISE	"Rejoice, the Lord is King"	Darwall
WORDS OF WELCOME		
SCRIPTURE READING	Isaiah 53:1-7,12; Luke 23:33-34;	
	I John 2:1; Hebrews 7:25	

HYMN OF CHRIST OUR SAVIOR

"Angels, from the Realms of Glory"		Regent Square
CALL TO PRAYER		Pastoral Prayer
THE MORNING OFFERING		
Anthem	"I Saw the Cross of Jesus"	Arr. Mayfield
	Choir	
Doxology		
Prayer of Dedication		

SERMON   "The Lord's Presence—in Heaven"

"Who has believed what we have heard? And to whom has the arm of the Lord been revealed? For he grew up before him like a young plant, and like a root out of dry ground; he had no form or comeliness that we should look at him, and no beauty that we should desire him. He was despised and rejected by men; a man of sorrows, and acquainted with grief; and as one from whom men hide their faces he was despised, and we esteemed him not. Surely he has borne our griefs and carried our sorrows; yet we esteemed him stricken, smitten by God, and afflicted. But he was wounded for our transgressions, he was bruised for our iniquities; upon him was the chastisement that made us whole, and with his stripes we are healed. All we like sheep have gone astray; we have turned every one to his own way; and the Lord has laid on him the iniquity of us all. He was oppressed, and he was afflicted, yet he opened not his mouth; like a lamb that is led to the slaughter, and like a sheep that before its shearers is dumb, so he opened not his mouth." (Isa. 53:1-7).

"Therefore I will divide him a portion with the great, and he shall divide the spoil with the strong; because he poured out his soul to death, and was numbered with the transgressors;/yet he bore the sin of many, and made intercession for the transgressors." (Isa. 53:12).

"And when they came to the place which is called The Skull, there they crucified him, and the criminals, one on the right and one on the left. And Jesus said, 'Father, forgive them; for they know not what they do.' And they cast lots to divide his garments." (Luke 23:33-34).

"Consequently he is able for all time to save those who draw near to God through him, since he always lives to make intercession for them." (Heb. 7:25).

In the Middle Ages, a popular preacher announced an evening sermon on the love of God. The congregation gathered early. Evening shadows lengthened. The last sunlight faded from the stained-glass windows.

The preacher entered the church carrying a large candle. He walked to a life-sized figure of Christ on the cross. The preacher silently held the light beneath the wounds in the Lord's feet; next, His hands, side, and thorn-pierced brow. Then he went out. The silent sermon left some worshipers weeping at the love of God which is beyond words.

In the Lord's Supper, silent but powerful symbols portray God's love for us. Christ died "for many."

God is in heaven. The Lord's Prayer teaches this. This means God is holy; God is transcendent—above us. He is not our peer. However, while God is not *one of us,* He is *one with us.* Jesus shared our humanity. Therefore, heaven knows and understands.

To say God is in heaven means He is powerful—in ultimate control of the world. He is Lord of the world and of eternity.

Therefore, we can be courageous. We have nothing ultimately to fear. As Elijah observed at Dothan, "Those who are with us are more than those who are with them" [the enemy] (2 Kings 6:16). The hills are alive with the hosts of heaven. We are not alone.

We can have assurance. For God who began a good work of redemption in us will see it to completion (see Phil. 1:6). God is in heaven; be glad!

Christ is in heaven, our Intercessor. He has carried humanity into the Godhead. He has nearest access to the Father. Isaiah promised that he would make "intercession for the transgressors" (53:12). Luke tells us about His intercession, even for His executioners, from the cross. The author of Hebrews wrote, "He always lives to make intercession" for us (7:25). In 1 John 2:1 we read, "We have an advocate with the Father"—a friend in heaven.

One day *we will be in heaven,* too. "For we know that if the earthly tent we live in is destroyed, we have a building from God, a house not made with hands, eternal in the heavens" (2 Cor. 5:1). We can believe in personal immortality. One day Jesus will beckon to us, "Come, ye blessed of my Father, inherit the kingdom prepared for you from the foundation of the world" (Matt. 25:34, KJV).

What will heaven be like? We have no blueprints but some precious glimpses. Heaven will be paradise—Eden restored. It will be the city of God, the New Jerusalem where God is forever present. There will be no night there: no night of pain and sorrow, sin, death, or separation. The risen Christ said, "Behold, I make all things new" (Rev.

21:5). That will include a new body, whole and complete like his post-resurrection body.

God is present in heaven, and so is Christ. One day we will be in heaven also—all who believe in Christ. Let us celebrate the divine Presence as we observe the Lord's Supper.

OBSERVANCE OF THE LORD'S SUPPER
   Giving of the Bread

"Meditation"   Hopson
Handbell Choir

   Giving of the Cup

"Surely He Hath Borne Our Griefs"   Graun
Ensemble

HYMN OF INVITATION "Breathe on Me, Breath of God" Jackson
SHARING OF DECISIONS   Benediction
MOMENT OF SILENCE   Organ Dismissal

7
In Events

PRELUDE
HYMN   "Down at the Cross"   Stockton
HYMN   "The Old Rugged Cross"   Bennard
WELCOME AND PRAYER
THE EVENING OFFERING
   Offertory
   Offertory Prayer
HYMN   "Moment by Moment"   Moody

SERMON   "The Lord's Presence—In Events"

"In many and various ways God spoke of old to our fathers by the prophets; but in these last days he has spoken to us by a Son, whom he appointed the heir of all things, through whom also he created the world." (Heb. 1:1-2).

"That which was from the beginning, which we have heard, which we have seen with our eyes, which we have looked upon and touched with our hands, concerning the word of life—the life was made manifest, and we saw it, and testify to it, and proclaim to you the eternal life which was with the Father and was made manifest to us—that which we have seen and heard we proclaim also to you, so that you may have fellowship with us; and our fellowship is with the Father and with his Son Jesus Christ." (1 John 1:1-3).

Christianity is an historical faith. Church historian Martin Marty considers this a well-kept secret. The God who created time, who existed before the beginning, entered time. Thus, history became what theologians have called "salvation history."

Thus, Christians are not custodians of antiquities, museum keepers, or tour guides to the city of the dead! Biblical faith stretches across more than two hundred centuries. It is ten times as old as the United States, and it is a living experience with God.

The God of history is a living God, still active in current events. George Buttrick described the normalization of relations between the US and China by exclaiming, "Look what God did with a Ping-Pong ball!"

God is present in the *great events*. There have been many "mighty acts of God." These include such events as the call of Abraham and Moses, the Exodus from Egypt, the conquest of Canaan, the rule of King David, and later Israel's return from Exile.

The Christ-event was God's mightiest act. It included Jesus' birth, ministry, death, and resurrection. Since Pentecost and the birth of the church, God has been accomplishing the redemption of humanity. Across the centuries, the church of Jesus Christ has grown from a handful to a billion souls who love His name today in the earth.

God is not simply present in the great events. He is also present in our *personal providence*. We are most often aware of the divine Presence at the "common ventures" of life.

God is present at the *birth* of a child. No one can witness that mystery without being impressed at its miraculous nature. God still "makes babies." At a parent dedication service, a new mother prayed for God's guidance "until one day we place their hand in yours."

God is present with us throughout *childhood*. Those are precious formative years. Jesus "took a child" and taught us to be trusting and teachable.

God is present when we go through the trauma of *adolescence*. It is an in-between time, a time of growth toward independence. A friend of mine says the only thing harder than being a teenager is having one. I've done both, and I agree. Parents are to give their children two things: roots and wings.

God is surely present with us in *adulthood*. This is the longest and most demanding stage of life. These have been called the "taffy years" when we are pulled in different directions. Some people snap!

Vance Havner prayed that God will let us get "home before dark." God is present in events glorious, tragic, and routine. Thanks be, "we cannot drift beyond His love and care."

God is present in the great events of salvation history. More than that, He is present to us in the great and ordinary events of our own lives.

The Lord's Supper brings us back to basics—reminding us of the Christ-event. Come, let us observe His command to remember Him, with great joy!

OBSERVANCE OF THE LORD'S SUPPER
    Giving of the Bread
    Giving of the Cup
HYMN   "Rock of Ages"   Hastings
SHARING OF DECISIONS   Benediction
MOMENT OF SILENCE   Organ Dismissal

8
In Suffering

SACRED ORGAN MUSIC "Lord Jesus Christ Be Present Now" Bach

CALL TO WORSHIP

HYMN   "Come, Thou Fount of Every Blessing"   Warrenton
   "Let Thy grace, Lord, like a fetter,
   bind my wand'ring heart to thee."

WORDS OF WELCOME

CALL TO PRAYER   Pastoral Prayer

THE MORNING OFFERING

   Offertory   "Hymne a Sainte Cecile"   Gounod
                       Violin and Piano

   Congregational Response   Barnby
      We give thee by Thine own,/ Whate'er the gift may be;
      All that we have is Thine along,/ A trust, O Lord, from Thee.

RESPONSIVE READING

   Pastor: When the church of Jesus/shuts its outer door,/ Lest the
               roar of traffic/ Drown the voice of prayer:/ May our
               prayers, Lord, make us/ Ten times more aware.

   People: That the world we banish/ Is our Christian care.

   Pastor: If our hearts are lifted/ Where devotion soars/ High
               above this hungry/ Suff'ring world of ours:/Lest our
               hymns should drug us/ To forget its needs,

   People: Forge our Christian worship/ Into Christian deeds.

   Pastor: Lest the gifts we offer,/ Money, talents, time,/Serve to
               salve our conscience/ To our secret shame:/Lord, re-
               prove, inspire us/ By the way you give;

   People: Teach us, dying Savior,/ How true Christians live.
               Amen.

Hymn   "O Thou to Whose All-Searching Sight"

Sermon   "The Lord's Presence—In Suffering"

Paul Tournier of Switzerland read an article entitled, "Orphans
Lead the World." It cited the large number of men and women having
achieved distinction in many fields who are orphans. Tournier is an
orphan himself. He concluded that deprivation and "creative suffering" can lead to unusual courage and creativity. Such was true on
occasion in the early church. The apostle Paul wrote to the church
in Philippi:

"Only, let your conduct be worthy of the gospel of Christ, so that whether
I come and see you for myself or hear about you from a distance, I may know
that you are standing firm, one in spirit, one in mind, contending as one man
for the gospel faith, meeting your opponents without so much as a tremor.
This is a sure sign to them that their doom is sealed, but a sign of your
salvation, and one afforded by God himself; for you have been granted the
privilege not only of believing in Christ but also of suffering for him. You and
I are engaged in the same contest; you saw me in it once, and, as you hear,
I am in it still." (Phil. 1:27-30, NEB).

"Let your conduct be worthy of the gospel" is a call to lead a
worthy life-style. Philippi was a Roman colony settled by retired
soldiers. Though it was miles from Rome they used Latin, and their
customs, dress, and culture were Roman. They were proud citizens
of the Empire.

In much the same way, Christians are citizens of the kingdom of
God. Therefore, we are to live worthily of the gospel we profess.
Paul's counsel is that we stand firmly by our standards. We are not
to live by the world's values, but by the Christian ethic. Stand firm
against the inroads of evil.

Many believers in the early church endured persecution. Christianity was an illegal religion in much of the Roman Empire for some
three hundred years. Christians endured torture, and many were

executed under the authority of the state. Standing firm in the faith was not an academic matter for them. It was practical and with predictable consequences.

There are places in the modern world where Christians are actively persecuted and suffer for their faith. It is costly for them to stand firm. More likely, the enemies with whom we have to contend are temptation to sin, the mystery of suffering, and coping with the reality of death.

The church must stand united against evil with "one Spirit" and "one mind"—unafraid. We know that evil is ultimately doomed to defeat, and we are destined for salvation. Paul's view was that the Christian life is a struggle, and suffering for Christ is a privilege. It affords the opportunity for us to do something for Jesus who gave His life for us.

Suffering Is Unavoidable

We are made of clay. That means suffering is an inescapable part of our humanity. We are creatures "from dust to dust returning." We are eventually subject to all the "slings and arrows of an outrageous fortune that flesh is heir to."

There are many ways in which people suffer. These include such as unemployment, poverty, and hunger. There are still millions of homeless refugees in the world. Every war has produced a host of them. We also suffer disappointment, failure, and loneliness. The loss of health, the loss of a loved one, and the loss of a purpose in living cause untold pain. It is also hurtful to endure criticism and being misunderstood. These are the sort of "arrows" we can all experience. No one is exempt from suffering—not even Jesus. Death is the ultimate privation.

Why Do We Suffer?

Sometimes it is due to our own unwise choices. We may bring the problem on ourselves. At other times, we may suffer because of what others do to us. We may be betrayed by a friend or a mate, or we may be injured by a drunken driver or a mugger.

We cannot always answer the "why" of tragedy or premature

death. Such suffering is often shrouded in mystery, and we have to admit we simply do not understand. There are some tragic events which we have trouble calling the will of God, because we know His will for us is good. We have to believe that the Heavenly Father is as brokenhearted as we are when tragic events occur.

How We Respond to Suffering . . .

. . . is of primary importance. We obviously cannot avoid all suffering. It is a real part of life, soon or late. However, we can avoid feeling sorry for ourselves when tragedy comes. Such experiences can make us bitter or better. How we respond determines which it will be. Usually we take one of three attitudes.

• We may rebel, shake our puny fists in the face of the Almighty, and cry, "Unfair!" Some people blame God when suffering comes.

• We may accept our suffering with a sense of resignation, stoically. Many go through life with a whining attitude saying, "Woe is me!"

• Paul taught us to rejoice in adversity. That is not easy, and such an attitude certainly is not automatic. It requires both faith and our best efforts. Our faith and trust are in God. Therefore, we believe even when we cannot fully understand that "in all things God is working for our good" (see Rom. 8:28).

Actually, we can learn from what we suffer. Wayne Oates wrote in his autobiography about his struggle to be free from ignorance and poverty. With feelings of inferiority, he grew up in a cotton mill village. He was practically fatherless. In his youth he knew loneliness, hunger, and distrust of those in authority. Oates also experienced prolonged pain through a series of back surgeries which were not successful. Still, he has gone on to become a leading scholar and pioneer in the field of pastoral care. He has contributed a major body of literature to that academic discipline. He has overcome the handicaps of earlier years and, despite them, has made a superb contribution. How we react or respond to what happens to us is of the utmost importance.

Remember that the Lord's Supper is about suffering. There had to be a cross and its agony before there could be the glory of Easter and resurrection. The Supper reminds us of the Suffering Servant of God,

His pain and death which atoned for our sin. Recall Tournier's conclusion: deprivation can lead to courage and creativity—it is not automatic but it is possible.

Come, let us observe this ordinance in remembrance of One who suffered! The Lord is with us!

OBSERVANCE OF THE LORD'S SUPPER
  Giving of the Bread
    Anthem   "The Eyes of All Wait upon Thee"   Berger
  Giving of the Cup
    Solo   "I Gave My Life for Thee"   Manuel
HYMN   "When I Survey the Wondrous Cross"   Mason
SHARING OF DECISIONS   Benediction
MOMENT OF SILENCE   Organ Dismissal

9
Abounding Love

SACRED ORGAN MUSIC
CALL TO WORSHIP
HYMN   "Love Divine, All Loves Excelling"   Zundel
WORDS OF WELCOME
CALL TO PRAYER   Pastoral Prayer
HYMN   "Jesus, Thy Boundless Love to Me"   Hemy
THE MORNING OFFERING
  Anthem   Romans 11:33-36   Danner
                Choir
  Congregational Response
All things are Thine; no gift have we,/
Lord of all gifts, to offer Thee;/
And hence, with grateful hearts today,/
Thine own before Thy feet we lay. Amen.   Bach

RESPONSIVE READING

Leader: Thou has multiplied, O Lord, Thy wondrous deeds and
             Thy thoughts toward us; none can compare with Thee!

People: We have thought on Thy steadfast love, O God, in the
             midst of They temple.

Leader: Because Thy steadfast love is better than life, my lips
             will praise Thee; I will bless Thee as long as I live.

People: Blessed be the Lord, our God, from everlasting to ever-
             lasting! Amen and Amen.[8]

SERMON   "The Lord's Presence—Abounding Love"

Let us listen to the Word of God in the Epistle to the Philippians:
1:9-11. The Book of Philippians is a gracious thank-you note from the
pen of the apostle Paul to a congregation whom he loved dearly. These
verses are the apostle's prayer:

"It is my prayer that your love may abound more and more, with knowledge and all discernment, so that you may approve what is excellent, and may
be pure and blameless for the day of Christ, filled with the fruits of righteousness which come through Jesus Christ, to the glory and praise of God."

This is an apostolic prayer. Wouldn't it be wonderful if, as we
prepare to gather at the Lord's table, we might have an apostle come
and pray for us. What splendid preparation that would be. What an
encouragement that would be, to have Paul pray for us and prepare
us to come to the Lord's table.

That is precisely what our text is, an apostolic prayer for the
Christians in Philippi and for us here. He asks these simple blessings
for us. In verse 9, that we might have *abounding love,* overflowing
love, growing love. That is a wonderful prayer. He didn't pray that
we might have more members. He didn't pray that we might subscribe
to the church budget. He didn't pray that we might be effective in our
missions outreach. His first prayer for the church in Philippi and
other churches was that they might experience abounding love.

Listen! "It is my prayer that your love may abound more and more." The equivalent of the abundant life which we have in Christ is the abounding love which we have for one another. There are many kinds of love in our world. Even animals can show devotion. There is also the love of a man for a maid.

The apostle is talking about a kind of love far grander than mere human love. He is writing about *agape* love, God's love. It is the kind of love that sent His only Son to die that unspeakable death in our place, that we might be forgiven and know the glory of salvation.

Agape love is the opposite of self-centeredness. It is unselfish, putting others first. I remember hearing a friend say, "You are first after me." That is not *agape* love. Agape love wills their highest good—even the highest good of our enemies. Do we love like that?

Paul prays for us, as we approach the table, that we might have this abounding love, this supreme gift—and that we might have it with *knowledge.* Christian love is intelligent love. It's not like cupid—blind. It's wide-eyed, intelligent, and caring.

He wants us to have this love with knowledge and discernment so we can have the ability to choose not merely between right and wrong, not just between good and evil, but between what is good and what is best. Sometimes we allow something good to become an enemy of the best.

Oh, that we might love more deeply, that we might love more intensely, that we might love more broadly—that is abounding love with knowledge. Love is one of the few things in this world of which it may be said: "The more you give away, the more you have."

Think of this as you prepare to partake of the Supper. The apostle is praying for us that we might have abounding love. And in verse 10, he prayed that we might have a sense of discernment: "that you may approve what is excellent." Moffatt translates this verse, "enabling you to have a sense of what is vital." How much time we waste on that which doesn't really matter! We focus ten billion brain cells on a two-bit problem or on an object with a low priority. We fret over minutia and neglect the matters that mean the most.

Parents of young children, think about it for a moment. You may fuss at a child for an aggravation and forget to make sure the child knows he or she is loved. May God give us the sense of what is vital. A couple, once excitedly and enthusiastically in love with each other, can come to that stage in their marriage where they take each other for granted. What sin against a relationship could be worse than that? May God give us a sense of what is vital, what matters most, what is really important. Let us not spend our best energies on baubles that actually don't matter.

May this sense of "what is vital" make you "pure and blameless for the day of the Christ," was the apostle's prayer. The word *pure* here is one which was used of refining gold ore. There were gold mines near Philippi. The miners would take the ore, melt it, and burn off the dross. I've read that those who are refining gold know it is pure when they can look into it and see their reflection. May you have that kind of purity, that kind of blamelessness, so you may sense what is vital. May your life be characterized by the ring of the real that you may be a spiritually authentic person.

I was a teenager when the soldiers were coming home from World War II. I worked at a soda fountain in Atlanta. A lot of foreign money was being passed. Boys were bringing home coins from other parts of the world and trying to buy a soft drink with it. In the back of the cash register was a little drawer filled with foreign coins.

About this time, someone in the Atlanta area made a mold in which they were making lead half-dollars. Several lead half-dollars were in that cash register drawer. When business was slack, I used to enjoy getting one of those half-dollars out and, along with a real, silver half-dollar, dropping them on the marble counter. There is a vast difference between lead and silver. One has the ring of the real; the other does not.

The passage from Philippians provides a beautiful prayer for us: that we might be able to discern what is vital; to approve what is excellent; that there might be about your life and mine the ring of the authentic. May God answer that prayer for us, that we might be prepared for the living of these days and for the Day of the Lord, when you and I will stand in the presence of the Almighty and give an account of the stewardship of life. On that Day, may we ring as that which is real.

Abounding Love   **41**

Hear the prayer again: that we might have a sense of what is vital, that we might have abounding love, and finally, in verse 11, that we might bear "the fruits of righteousness." That phrase calls to mind Paul's phrase in Galatians 5:22-23, in which he lists the fruit of the Spirit—there are nine of them.

The first three have to do with our relationship with God. They are love, joy, and peace. In relationship to others we are to have patience, kindness, and goodness. Finally, three gifts relate to ourselves—faithfulness, gentleness, and self-control. When the French Bible translates the Beatitude "Blessed are the meek" it reads: "Blessed are the debonair"—God's gentle people who have self-control and who live under God's control.

The apostle ended that Galatian passage by explaining, "Against such there is no law" (v. 23). No legislature ever passed a law against love, joy, and inner peace or against patience, kindness, goodness, faithfulness, gentleness, and self-control. Love makes the difference; it makes all the difference in the world.

I have a friend who grew up on "the wrong side of the tracks" in a small town. One Sunday afternoon, some youth from the First Baptist Church went visiting in that area. They invited this friend and some other boys to come to Training Union. He decided to go, not to see what it was like, but to make fun of the boys at the First Baptist Church.

He went, and it wasn't at all what he had expected. He felt a warmth and acceptance. He was attracted there, and he went back. He became a Christian. I heard him report, with a tinge of sorrow in his voice, that the four best friends with whom he grew up all came to grief. One died by his own hand. Another, convicted of a felony, went to prison. Another was executed for murder, and the fourth one was put in the insane asylum.

Love makes a difference. The apostle prays for us as we come to the table, that we might have abounding love, and that's what the Lord's Supper is about.

OBSERVANCE OF THE LORD'S SUPPER
  Giving of the Bread
    Solo   "Jesus Paid It All"   Young
  Giving of the Cup
    Anthem   "Jesus, Thou Joy of Loving Hearts" Baker/Fultz
               Choir and Soloist
HYMN   "O Love of God Most Full"   Jackson
SHARING OF DECISIONS   Benediction
MOMENT OF SILENCE   Organ Dismissal

10
In Self-Examination

PRELUDE
HYMN   "At the Cross"   Hudson
WELCOME AND PRAYER
HYMN   "I Stand Amazed in the Presence"   Gabriel
RESPONSIVE READING   Psalm 51
SERMON HYMN   "O Thou to Whose All-Searching Sight"
                              Words Zinzendorf

SERMON   "The Lord's Presence—In Self-Examination"

The Scots call their capital Edinburgh, "auld reekie." It sounds like a put-down, but it is really a term of affection. Since the Industrial Revolution, Edinburgh has been a smoky city except on the Sunday when the fires are banked.

The Lord's Supper is a time when we clear the dust from our busy lives, a time to come aside and be still and know that He is God, a time to let the clouds of theological doubts be dispelled. It calls us back to the rudiments, back to center.

We can argue all kinds of niceties of theological difference, but the Lord's Supper keeps directing us back to home base. It reminds us of the cross and our salvation. The Supper never lets us lose sight of the most central teaching of our faith. At the observance of the Lord's Supper we are standing on holy ground. It is a place where things come clear—a place where Christ is present.

As we prepare to take these bits of broken bread and this cup in remembrance of Him, let us precede our worship experience by a time of personal self-examination, for the private confession of our sins.

Let us confess to God our wrong attitudes, our vaulting pride that "o'er leaps itself and falls on the other." Let us confess our sense of superiority to others, because we may have more education or because we may have more money or possessions. We are proud in an unhealthy sense. We arrogantly look down on other people. Let us confess to God our sin of pride, for it has jaundiced our relationships. We tend to despise those who are different from us.

In the Sermon on the Mount, Jesus taught many truths which we can read in a single sitting. Jesus declared, "You have heard it said, 'You shall do no murder,' but I say to you, don't hate your brother." Further, "You have heard it said of old, 'You shall not commit adultery,' but I say to you, beware the lustful look." And further, "You have read of old, 'You shall love your friends and hate your enemies,' but I say to you, Love your enemies. Pray for those who persecute and despitefully use you" (author's paraphrase on Matt. 5:21ff). The radical ethics and theology of Jesus need to be taken seriously. They constitute a call to repentance.

Jesus taught that if we keep the wrong attitudes out of our minds and hearts we will exclude the wrong actions out of our lives. Hatred leads to murder, the lustful look, to adultery. And hating our enemies instead of loving them leads to all kinds of hostility, violence, and war. Jesus goes behind the deed to the attitude from which it grows.

Let us repent of wrong attitudes. Let us repent of wrong actions, for we are guilty of both. Our selfishness always looks out for number one. It never truly takes another person into account, unless it is somehow for our benefit. God forgive us.

We are often inconsiderate of others and hurt them. We forget others who are in need. A group on a mission trip to Ecuador was struck by the sharp contrast between all we have and the utter poverty in which other people, our neighbors, live.

May God forgive us not only for what we've done that is wrong but also for our sins of neglect. We are guilty of ingratitude, and we are uncaring. We fail to encourage others and to help them. Remember that line in the Lord's Prayer: "Forgive us our debts,/As we also have forgiven our debtors" (Matt. 6:12). Let us examine our hearts in light of that petition.

May we also find encouragement at the Lord's Table. We can have assurance of divine forgiveness and grace. The Lord is "a very present help in time of trouble." If you are confused and trying to make a decision, listen to Jesus. He said, "I am the way, the truth, and the life" (John 14:6). Follow Him. Ask the Lord for His guidance, for His direction, here at the table.

Doubtless there are some here who are carrying the guilt of unconfessed and unforgiven sins. Hear the words of Jesus; the words of Scripture: "If we confess our sins, he is faithful and just to forgive us our sins, and to cleanse us from all unrighteousness" (1 John 1:9, KJV). Claim that Scripture promise, and you can go out of this room a different person than you came in.

There are some here who are troubled and anxious. Hear this marvelous text: "Cast all your anxieties on him, for he cares about you" (1 Pet. 5:7). Try it. It is highly practical. It is a powerful promise. It is authentic. Believe, and you shall see.

There are some here who have come with a burden. It may not be obvious, but you have a burden in your heart. Maybe it's an unresolved grief you haven't finished working through. Maybe it's a "secret" nobody else in all the world knows, not even your mate or your dearest friend. But you're carrying that unseen burden like sackcloth beneath your clothing. Then hear the words of the Lord: "Come unto me, all ye that labour and are heavy laden, and I will give you rest" (Matt. 11:28, KJV).

Then there are the bored. Life today was so much like yesterday, and tomorrow won't be much different. You are bored to tears. You've lost your sense of purpose and direction. Then hear the challenge of Jesus, "As the Father has sent me, even so I send you" (John 20:21). Look about and discover your gifts. Find your personal ministry. What would the Lord have you do?

We have a neighbor who is eighty-two. He looks after the people who live on his block. He puts out the garbage for some ladies who cannot. He takes in the mail for a family across the street who is in Europe. He sees to the sick who live on his block. He has a beautiful personal ministry to his neighbors, when you'd expect somebody to be ministering to him.

Maybe you are carrying a burden of grief. Then hear the words of Jesus, "I will not leave you comfortless: I will come to you" (John 14:18, KJV).

Whatever your need, there is an answer from the Christ. Oh, maybe not the answer to the question "Why?" Maybe it is not the answer you are looking for, but you are not left alone in the midst of any need. We have Christ's presence and grace.

As you come to examine your heart, join me in confessing our sins of attitude, action, and neglect, but also join me in finding encouragement in the Scriptures. Finally, in preparation for the Lord's Supper, let me remind you that at heart the Lord's Supper is a Thanksgiving feast. Jesus "took the cup and gave thanks" [*eucharistia*]. He took the cup and gave thanks.

Oh, how much we have for which to be thankful! Let me simply list a few blessings: you can add to the list. Food—trustworthy food and drugs—we don't have to wonder if something is sanitary or safe. Freedom—we are free to come and free to go. We are free to vote. We live in a land where we choose those who govern us. Do you know how rare that is in the world? Freedom.

Forgiveness—ah, that's the heart of our faith. Where would we be without divine forgiveness? Work to do and usefulness, what a blessing! Love—if there is someone in the earth whom you love and if there is someone in the world who loves you, you are rich, my friend, rich beyond measure.

Scripture—where would we be without our Guidebook? The church—the fellowship of the redeemed—where would we be without the encouragement and support and prayers of those who are our kinsfolk in Christ? The Bible, the church, the Holy Spirit—God has provided us an abundance for which we are grateful.

What is one thing you are most grateful for? Health, family, freedom of worship—the list goes on.

A tornado hit the city where I served my first church. They called out the National Guard to prevent looting. We went to a Sunday evening service, and there was a guardsman standing in the driveway of my church, waving the cars past because the church was on the edge of the area where the tornado had struck. The sight sent a chill up my spine! There could be an armed soldier standing every Sunday at the entrance to our meeting house, waving away those who would come in. Thank God for freedom of worship.

Christian parents—what a heritage they gave us. Life itself—all of life is the gift of God. Friends, genuine friends, are a cherished gift as well.

What are you grateful for?

God provides for our salvation; He paid our sin debt at Calvary, and we've been forgiven. We celebrate His Presence with us in the observance of the Lord's Supper, and God gives us the hope of immortality. This life is not all there is. *Glory* awaits. Some of us have friends and loved ones on the other side. One day we shall be with them and be with the Lord, and it will be glory indeed!

Self-examination precedes our coming to the Lord's Table. It's a time for confession, for the assurance of forgiveness, and for thanksgiving. Like Jesus, let us take the bread and the cup and give thanks.

"As often as you eat this bread and drink the cup, you proclaim the Lord's death until he comes" (2 Cor. 11:26).

ORDINANCE OF THE LORD'S SUPPER
   Giving of the Bread
      Solo   "Search Me, O God"   Hopkins
   Giving of the Cup
      Anthem   "Create in Me a Clean Heart, O God"   Mueller

Choir
HYMN   "More Love to Thee, O Christ"   Doane
SHARING OF DECISIONS   Benediction
MOMENT OF SILENCE   Organ Dismissal

11
In Crisis

SACRED ORGAN MUSIC
                    "Andante in D Minor"   Walond
                    "Auf meinen lieben Gott"   Hanff
CHIMING OF THE HOUR
INVOCATION AND THE LORD'S PRAYER
HYMN   "Rejoice, the Lord is King"   Darwall
CALL TO PRAYER   Pastoral Prayer
HYMN   "In the Cross of Christ I Glory"   Conkey
THE MORNING OFFERING
    Anthem   Romans 11:33-36
O the depths of the riches, both of the wisdom and knowledge of God!
How unfathomable are His decisions, and His ways untraceable! For
who has known the mind of the Lord, or who His counselor ever
became? Or who has given to Him and God still owes Him the debt?
O the depths of the riches, both of the wisdom and knowledge of God
to Him be the glory through all the ages.
    Congregational Response
        Bless Thou the gifts our hands have bro't;
        Bless Thou the work our hearts have planned;
            Ours is the faith, the will, the tho't;
            The rest, O God, is in Thy hand. Amen. Schumann
RESPONSIVE READING
    Leader: Know ye that the Lord he is God:

People: it is he that hath made us, and not we ourselves; we are his people, and the sheep of his pasture.

Leader: Enter into his gates with thanksgiving, and into his courts with praise: be thankful unto him, and bless his name. Ps. 100

SERMON   "The Lord's Presence—In Crisis"

God is everywhere. There is no place where He is not present, except in hell. The essence of hell is the absence of God, separation of the soul from its Maker.

The author of Psalm 139:7-12 tried to escape God's omnipresence but discovered that he could not:

Whither shall I go from thy Spirit?
  Or whither shall I flee from thy presence?
If I ascend to heaven, thou are there!
If I make my bed Sheol, thou are there!
If I take the wings of the morning
  and dwell in the uttermost parts of the sea,
even there thy hand shall lead me,
  and thy right hand shall hold me.
If I say, "Let only darkness cover me,
  and the light about me be night,"
even the darkness is not dark to thee,
  the night is bright as the day;
  for darkness is as light with thee.

Francis Thompson described inescapable divine Presence as "the hound of heaven" with feet that "follow, follow after."

The divine Presence which is every place is focused in our worship. John Calvin would call this "Word and Sacrament," Scripture and the ordinances. God encounters us, and we are never again the same.

Consider three encounters with God recorded in the Scriptures:

Jacob and his mother Rebekah tricked his blind father Isaac and stole his elder brother Esau's inheritance. Then enroute to Haran to find a bride, Jacob unexpectedly encountered the Almighty. Listen to what happened (Read Gen. 28:10-19).

Using a stone for a pillow, Jacob dreamed of a ladder which reached from earth to heaven—with angels going up and down it. The ladder is a reminder of God's providential care, through the ministry of His angels. It also foreshadows the incarnation—that night when God himself came down the ladder at Bethlehem with a baby on his arm.

Jacob's experience was awe inspiring. "Surely the Lord is in this place; and I knew it not. . . . This is none other but the house of God, and this is the gate of heaven" (KJV). Jacob named the place Beth-el, house of God. He set up a stone pillar and worshiped God there.

Isaiah was a sensitive young man who was grieving at the death of his friend King Uzziah. At worship in the Temple, he had a vision and heard the call of God. Listen: (Read Isa. 6:1-8). Isaiah felt unworthy. His lips were purified with a coal from the altar. He gave a ready answer to God's call, unlike Moses who was hesitant.

To see this third cameo of encounter, listen to the account in Luke 24:13-35. The risen Christ walked beside them on the seven-mile journey from Jerusalem to Emmaus. They recognized Him in the breaking of bread.

Notice these observations about the three encounters.

1. They occurred to very different people.

Jacob was a crook, a trickster. He was a sinner unworthy of divine grace (so are we). Isaiah was a young aristocrat, a courtier at the king's palace. The two at Emmaus were a couple of Jesus' disciples.

2. They occurred at very different places.

Jacob met the Lord at a campsite. Isaiah encountered Him at worship in the Temple in Jerusalem. Those at Emmaus realized they were in the presence of Christ at their dinner table. I dedicated a book on the Lord's Supper to my parents: "To Howard Banks and Opal Oxford McEachern in whose home I learned that Christ is Lord of the dinner table as well as Lord of the Communion Table."

3. The common denominator in these three encounters was crisis.

Jacob was fleeing the wrath of his brother, Esau. Isaiah was grieving the loss of his friend, King Uzziah. The two at Emmaus had experienced the death of their dearest friend and fondest dream. They confessed to Jesus, "We had hoped that he was the one to redeem Israel" (v. 21). Note the pathos of their crushed dream. All three encounters involved personal crisis. That is not the only way God comes to us, but it is one way. C. S. Lewis contended that God whispers in our pleasures but shouts in our pain.

The risen Christ is very much alive! And we are apt to meet Him in our worship at the table—a reminder of the crisis of the cross. Be sensitive to the divine Presence.

Hear His *claim* on us: "Follow me, and I will make you fishers of men" (Matt. 4:19).

Hear His *offer* to us: "If we confess our sins, He is faithful and just to forgive us our sins, and to cleanse us from all unrighteousness" (I John 1:9, KJV).

Be aware of His *presence* with us: "I will not leave you comfortless: I will come to you" (John 14:18, KJV).

OBSERVANCE OF THE LORD'S SUPPER
  Giving of the Bread
    Solo   "Christ, the Center"   Vick
  Giving of the Cup
    Chorale   "O Sacred Head, Now Wounded"   Arr. Bach
                                                       Tune: Hassler
HYMN   "Rock of Ages, Cleft for Me"   Hastings
SHARING OF DECISIONS
BENEDICTION   Moment of Silence   Organ Dismissal

12
In Times of Trouble

SACRED ORGAN MUSIC   "Prelude from the First Partita"   Bach
CALL TO WORSHIP

HYMN   "Joyful, Joyful, We Adore Thee"   Beethoven
WORDS OF WELCOME
HYMN   "Eternal Father, Strong to Save"   Dykes
Eternal Father, strong to save,/ Whose arm doth bind the restless
wave,/ Who bidd'st the mighty ocean deep/ Its own appointed limits
keep; O hear us when we cry to Thee/ For those in peril on the sea.
O Saviour, Whose almighty word/ The winds and waves submissive
heard, Who walked'st on the foaming deep,/ And calm amidst its rage
did sleep; O hear us when we cry to Thee,/ For those in peril on the
sea.
O Holy Spirit, Who didst brood/ Upon the waters dark and rude, And
bid their angry tumult cease,/ And give for wild confusion peace; O
hear us when we cry to Thee/ For those in peril on the sea.[9]
CALL TO PRAYER   Organ
THE MORNING PRAYER   Pastoral Prayer
   ANTHEM   "How Lovely Are Thy Dwellings"   Brahms
                              Choir
   Congregational Response
All things are Thine; no gift have we,
Lord of all gifts, to offer Thee;/
And hence with grateful hearts today,
Thine own before Thy feet we lay. Amen.

   Offertory Prayer

SERMON   "The Lord's Presence—In Times of Trouble"

   "On that day, when evening had come, he said to them, 'Let us go
across to the other side.' And leaving the crowd, they took him with
them in the boat just as he was, and other boats were with him. And
a great storm of wind arose, and the waves beat into the boat, so that
the boat was already filling. But he was in the stern, asleep on the
cushion; and they woke him and said to him, 'Teacher, do you not
care if we perish?' And he awoke and rebuked the wind, and said to
the sea, 'Peace! Be still!' And the wind ceased, and there was a great
calm. He said to them, 'Why are you afraid? Have you no faith?' And

they were filled with awe, and said to one another, 'Who then is this, that even wind and sea obey him?' " (Mark 4:35-41).

Some went down to the sea in ships,/doing business on the great waaters;/they saw the deeds of the Lord,/his wondrous works in the deep./For he commanded, and raised the stormy wind,/which lifted up the waves of the sea./They mounted up to heaven, they went down to the depths;/their courage melted away in their evil plight;/they reeled and staggered like drunken men,/and were at their wits' end./Then they cried to the Lord in their trouble,/and he delivered them from their distress;/he made the storm be still,/and the waves of the sea were hushed./Then they were glad because they had quiet,/and he brought them to their desired haven./Let them thank the Lord for his steadfast love,/for his wonderful works to the sons of men! (Ps. 107:23-31).

Seasickness is an unpleasant experience. A storm at sea can be frightening. The psalmist described it vividly. However, there are also other kinds of storms:

• Storms of doubt can assail us with considerable discomfort. Some may doubt their faith and even the presence of God. We may have cause to doubt the love and faithfulness of a mate. At times we question our own ability to cope with problems. We may not feel equal to our jobs, to our marriages, or to parenting.

• There are storms of anxiety and stress. We feel pulled apart by circumstances beyond our control. Fear paralyzes us until we cannot make decisions or choose correctly.

• Stormy times assault us when our health fails, or that of a loved one. We come up against our limitations, and we find this hard to accept.

• Grief and sorrow leave us tempest tossed. We feel like the character in *Green Pastures* who complained, "Everything dat's fastened down is coming loose!"[10]

Jesus, Saviour, pilot me
Over life's tempestuous sea.

It is time to claim the promises of Scripture: "When you pass through the waters I will be with you" (Isa. 43:2).

Recall the account of Jesus stilling the storm on the Sea of Galilee. Mark's account appears to be based on Simon Peter's remembrance of the event. Small details are recounted which must have come from an eyewitness. The storm was a sudden and raging tempest. The Greek word Mark employed to describe it is similar to the word for an earthquake. The boat was about to be swamped, and the disciples, who were experienced fishermen, were frightened. Hear their plea, "Do you not care if we perish?" (One night they would sleep when Jesus needed them to watch. But now he was asleep in the storm.)

Jesus rebuked the wind and waves. The literal Greek means, "Be muzzled!" And calm returned. The disciples were in awe: "Who then is this, that even the wind and sea obey him?" (v. 41). Their fear turned to faith.

Jesus had miracle power over nature. This is consistent with the incarnation—"God was in Christ" (2 Cor. 5:19, KJV). Raymond Brown wrote that a miracle may be an event which is contrary to nature—or it may be contrary to nature as we know and understand it. In the Bible, a miracle was an act of God on behalf of His people. Nature is not a closed system. There can be exceptions to what we know of natural laws. Supernatural intervention can occur. Yet, there is more than a nature miracle in this passage. Look to the larger truth.

The same Jesus who stilled the storm on Galilee is present with us today. He is with us in the stormy times of life and the calm ones; He is present when the going is rough and when it is great—and in the ordinary times as well. The storm may continue to rage, or it may grow calm, but we are not alone.

William Barclay lost his grown daughter in an accident at sea. Years later he would cite this passage and say to his students, "As he stilled the storm on Galilee, so he stills the storm in our hearts."

This passage from the Gospel of Mark is a call to faith. " 'Twas grace that taught my heart to fear,/And grace my fears relieved." What Jesus did for the disciples on the Sea of Galilee, He does for us. As surely as He was present with them, He is present with us.

There is powerful symbolism in these passages. The storm represents chaos overcome at creation. The deep stands for trouble, evil, whatever threatens us. The boat or ark is a biblical symbol of safety in the storm. It stands for the church in Christian art.

Whether we have smooth sailing or stormy seas, Christ is in the boat with us. We live in His Presence.

> Eternal Father, strong to save,
> Whose arm doth bind the restless wave,
> Who bidd'st the mighty ocean deep
> Its own appointed limits keep;
> O hear us when we cry to Thee
> For those in peril on the sea.

OBSERVANCE OF THE LORD'S SUPPER
    Giving of the Bread
        Solo   "Be Still, My Soul"   Sibelius
    Giving of the Cup
        Instrumental Meditation   "Jesus, Savior, Pilot Me"   Gould
HYMN   "O Love of God Most Full"   Jackson
SHARING OF DECISIONS
BENEDICTION
MOMENT OF SILENCE
ORGAN DISMISSAL

13
When We Are Tempted

PRELUDE
CALL TO WORSHIP
HYMN "Ask Ye What Great Thing I Know"   Schwedler (words)
                                           Hendon (tune)
WORDS OF WELCOME
SOLO "Is There Anything I Can Do For You?" Rambo/Huntsinger

SCRIPTURE READING   Selections from John
CALL TO PRAYER   Pastoral Prayer
HYMN   "I Saw the Cross of Jesus"   Whitfield
THE MORNING OFFERING
   Anthem   "O Divine Redeemer"   Gounod
Choir and Solo
   Congregational Response   Hew/Trentham
We give Thee but Thine own,
whate'er the gift may be,
All that we have is Thine alone,
a trust, O Lord, from Thee. Amen.
   Unison Reading
Grant us grace, our dear Father, to have before all things a vital
faith in Christ, an unshakable confidence in Thy mercy so we may
overcome the blindness of our erring conscience.

Give us a fervent love for Thee and for all mankind. Amen.

SERMON   "John's Portrait of Jesus"

"Blessed is the man who endures trial, for when he has stood the
test he will receive the crown of life which God has promised to those
who love him. Let no one say when he is tempted, "I am tempted by
God"; for God cannot be tempted with evil and he himself tempts no
one; but each person is tempted when he is lured and enticed by his
own desire. Then desire when it has conceived gives birth to sin; and
sin when it is full-grown brings forth death." (Jas. 1:12-15).

Temptation is as old as Adam. The Bible's word for temptation may
also be translated "test." Abraham's offer of his son Isaac was a test
of Abraham's faith.

The Source of Temptation

Temptation comes *from without*. It may be due to the evil influence
of other persons. Youth and adults know the social pressure of peers.

Robert Burns commented of a friend, "His friendship did me mischief."

Even though temptation comes from outside us, that does not give us license to blame our sins on someone else. We cannot pass the buck to society or the system or simply alibi, "The devil made me do it." We are still responsible for our actions—we responded to the temptations and gave in to them. Trying to blame someone else is simply a cop-out.

Part of the dark side of our nature is seen in the fact that we even blame God for the wrong we do. To quote Burns again: "Thou knowest thou hast formed me with passions wild and strong/And listening to their witching voices has often led me wrong."

In Homer's writings the character Agamemnon says, "It was not I that did it. Zeus and Fate struck me mad."

Blaming our sin on the Creator goes back as far as the Garden of Eden. Eve blamed the serpent for beguiling her. Adam blamed both Eve and his Maker for his sin. "The woman whom thou gavest to be with me, she gave me the fruit of the tree, and I ate" (Gen. 3:12). James disagreed. He wrote that God "tempts no one" (1:13)

Temptation also comes *from within*. Our desire responds to the appeal of the temptation. James further wrote, "Each person is tempted when he is lured and enticed by his own desire" (1:14). The word used here described an angler. A fisherman's bait is called a lure.

Actually, temptation is powerless until our desire responds to its overtures. A hungry person can be tempted by a steak, but not so if he has already eaten and has no desire for food.

Look at James's description of the anatomy of temptation: "Desire when it has conceived gives birth to sin; and sin when it is full-grown brings death" (1:15). The Greek word for "gives birth" is actually "whelps"—like an animal. Desire can be beastly, less than human.

We cherish and cultivate our desires. They are coddled, fondled, kept warm in our imagination and fantasy world. Be warned; they may produce a monster. To use another metaphor, desire is in the pit stop, gassed up and gunning the engine. It is waiting for the flag of temptation to drop, and it will hit the track.

Still, we are responsible for our actions. It is not a sin to be tempted, but we do not have to give in to the temptation.

The Way Out . . .

. . . is provided with every temptation. "No temptation has overtaken you that is not common to man. God is faithful, and he will not let you be tempted beyond your strength, but with the temptation will also provide the way of escape, that you may be able to endure it" (1 Cor. 10:13). The New Testament word for "way of escape" or way out is *ekbasis*. It was used of a mountain pass or crossing the Red Sea.

We do not have to yield to temptation. Joseph asked Potiphar's wife, "How then can I do this great wickedness, and sin against God?" (Gen. 39:9).

When temptation comes, remember your self-respect. Ernest Hemingway defined sin as "what you feel bad after." Remember that you have to live with yourself.

When temptation comes, remember those who love you; they have confidence in you and believe in you. You do not want to fail them, to betray them. Think of your wife or husband, your parents, children, or colleagues.

When temptation comes, remember that you belong to God. All our sins are ultimately against God (see Ps. 51:4). Our sins do not simply break God's law, they break His heart as well. We do not want to yield to temptation and disappoint the Lord.

Temptation can be resisted, and we will be stronger for it. When we yield to temptation and sin, others are hurt, we feel guilty, and we break God's heart. The gospel is that God sent Jesus to atone for our sins. When we repent, God forgives us, and we are restored to fellowship with the Father.

Remember, we are not alone in the time of temptation. God is present with us, and He provides an *ekbasis,* a way out.

OBSERVANCE OF THE LORD'S SUPPER
    Giving of the Bread
        Anthem   "The Eyes of All Wait Upon Thee"   Berger
    Giving of the Cup

Solo	"I Gave My Life for Thee"	Manuel
HYMN	"When I Survey the Wondrous Cross"	Mason
SHARING OF DECISIONS		Benediction
MOMENT OF SILENCE		Organ Dismissal

OBSERVANCE OF THE LORD'S SUPPER

Giving of the Bread

| Solo | "The Lord's Prayer" | Camilieri |

Giving of the Cup

Anthem	"In Remembrance"	Red
	Choir and Flute	
HYMN	"Jesus, Thou Joy of Loving Hearts"	Palmer/Quebec
BENEDICTION	Moment of Silence	Organ Dismissal

14
Answers Our Doubts

SACRED ORGAN MUSIC "Chorale Prelude on Vexilla Regis" Willan

CALL TO WORSHIP

| HYMN | "Rejoice, the Lord is King" | Darwall |

WORDS OF WELCOME

| CALL TO PRAYER | | Pastoral Prayer |
| HYMN | "The Church's One Foundation" | Wesley |

THE MORNING OFFERING AND FELLOWSHIP OFFERING

| Anthem | "Jesu, Word of God Incarnate" | Mozart |
| | Choir | |

Congregational Response

I've Found a Friend, O Such a Friend"   Words, Small
(Hymn: "The King of Love My Shepherd Is"; tune: DOMINUS
REGIT ME)

Naught that I have my own I call, I hold it for the Giver;

My heart, my strength, my life, my all, are His, and His forever. Amen.

RESPONSIVE READING

Leader: Remind us as we give, O Lord, of an open cross upon a lonely hill, where all the generosity and love of a compassionate heavenly Father culminated in the willing sacrifice of the obedient Son for our salvation.

People: Then may we give, humbled in gratitude, determined in generosity, and dedicated in commitment, to sacrifice in Thy service and live in Thy joy. Amen.[11]

SERMON   "The Lord's Presence—Answers Our Doubts"

"After these things the word of the Lord came to Abram in a vision, 'Fear not, Abram, I am your shield; your reward shall be very great.' But Abram said, 'O Lord God, what wilt thou give me, for I continue childless, and the heir of my house is Eliezer of Damascus?' And Abram said, 'Behold, thou hast given me no offspring; and a slave born in my house will be my heir.' And behold, the word of the Lord came to him, 'This man shall not be your heir; your own son shall be your heir.' And he brought him outside and said, 'Look toward heaven, and number the stars, if you are able to number them.' Then he said to him, 'So shall your descendants be.' And he believed the Lord; and he reckoned it to him as righteousness." (Gen. 15:1-6).

These are times which test our faith. All about us is a sea of secularism. Many are out to make a "fast buck." They are looking out for number one—no matter the harm to others. Recall automaker DeLorean's being accused of attempting to sell twenty-two million dollars worth of cocaine to rescue his bankrupt plant.

Corruption and greed are found in corporate board rooms and among assembly-line workers. Not even educators or churchgoers are immune.

Many persons face shattering personal crises: a fearful medical report, the agonizing loss of a loved one, loss of work with its threat to livelihood and human dignity.

Religious confusion abounds. Cults prey on naïve believers who are unsure of just what they do believe.

None of us know with certainty how we would stand the test. That is why Jesus taught us to pray: "Lead us not into temptation, But deliver us from evil" (Matt. 6:13). This phrase may be correctly translated: "Do not bring us to the test, but deliver us from the evil one"

Despite our faith and trust in God, we have moments of doubt. There are unanswered questions which loom large and shut out the sun of our faith.

Doubt Is Faith's Twin

One of the most honest prayers in the Bible is that of the father who said to Jesus, "I believe; Help thou my unbelief." (Mark 9:24, KJV). In all our faith, there is a strain of doubt. This is natural.

Abraham had received the bright promises of God: to bless him and, through his multitude of descendants, to bless humanity. (That promise was fulfilled in the person of Christ.) Childless Abraham believed God. Years passed, and still there was no heir. It appeared that he would have to adopt a slave to inherit his estate (and the promise). In Genesis 15, Abraham had obviously grown impatient. He was asking, "How can I be sure?" He received divine reassurance.

We want to know the future. That's why fortune-tellers, astrologers, and the writers of horoscopes prosper—with their vague answers and ambiguous hints. I've never believed in that sort of thing. I recall Soviet Premier Krushchev's visit to the United States. Jeane Dixon predicted that he would die at the hand of an assassin while in our country. He died years later in his sleep at his country villa outside Moscow. Yet people still pay attention, and papers publish these prognostications. We look foolish, don't we?

We cannot know the future. The best informed among us can only make an educated guess. I've read that the 1939 World's Fair focused on the world of the future—without the mention of jet aircraft! Be glad we do not know the future, for good or ill. Be glad our days are in His hands, and we walk by faith in daily trust.

Still, it gives certain comfort to realize that others have had their doubts, too. Abraham, Job, Thomas, and Paul all doubted as well as believed. It is noteworthy that Jesus did not put Thomas down for doubting—He merely affirmed, "Blessed are those who have not seen and yet believe" (John 20:29). (That is us!)

Doubt is not necessarily unhealthy. It can lead to an intelligent and devout faith. A student at Harvard University once said to George Buttrick, "I don't give a——about Jesus Christ." Buttrick replied, "Isn't it wonderful that He doesn't feel that way about you?"

Faith's Test

I believe First John 3 is the greatest chapter on the assurance of faith:

• The test of the heart (vv. 20-21). We can know we are right with God when "our hearts do not condemn us." Our sins have been confessed and forgiven. We have a clear conscience, and this gives us confidence toward God. Thomas á Kempis wrote that man looks on the deed, but God looks on the intention of the heart.

• The test of answered prayer (v. 22*a*). "We receive from him whatever what we ask," and this gives us assurance of our salvation. God answers our prayers. He does not always grant our requests, any more than wise parents give their children everything they ask. But God does answer our prayers, and this is encouraging. He has been with us in times past, and we are assured we can trust Him for the present and future.

• The test of obedience (v. 22*b*). We know we belong to God because "we keep his commandments and do what pleases him." The essence of sonship is obedience. Through obedience we can know we are the Heavenly Father's children.

A husband comes in from work. His wife says, "*Your son* is in his room upstairs!" The father may well ask, "When did he become *my* son instead of *our* son?" The answer is obvious—when he disobeyed his mother!

The children of God live in obedient faith.

• Ultimate assurance comes from the test of the Spirit (v. 24). "By this we know he abides in us, by the Spirit he has given us." Do your actions and reactions reflect the Spirit of Christ? Is the mind of Christ in you? This gives reason for assurance. A golden text is Romans 8:16: "The Spirit himself [bears] witness with our spirit that we are children of God."

The Lord's Supper is the symbol par excellence of His presence—and of our assurance. This observance is a sign of love made visible—God in flesh, incarnate.

Hear the Word of God in Paul's ringing doxology from Romans 8:

"If God is for us, who is against us?" (v. 31).

"Who shall separate us from the love of Christ? Shall tribulation, or distress, or persecution, or famine, or nakedness, or peril, or sword?" (v. 35).

"No, in all these things we are more than conquerors through him who loved us. For I am sure that neither death, nor life, nor angels, nor principalities, nor things present, nor things to come, nor powers, nor height, nor depth, nor anything else in all creation, will be able to separate us from the love of God in Christ Jesus our Lord" (vv. 37-39).

>Blessed assurance, Jesus is mine!
>Oh, what a foretaste of glory divine!

Come, let us gather at the Lord's table—in assurance of our salvation and with great joy!

OBSERVANCE OF THE LORD'S SUPPER
  Giving of the Bread
    Solo   "At Calvary"   Arr. Manuel
  Giving of the Cup
    Anthem   "Blessed Lord, All Love Excelling"   Liszt
HYMN   "More Love to Thee, O Christ"   Doane
SHARING OF DECISIONS   Benediction
MOMENT OF SILENCE   Organ Dismissal

15
At the End of Your Rope

SACRED ORGAN MUSIC   "Built on a Rock"   Manz
CALL TO WORSHIP
HYMN   "Praise to the Lord, the Almighty"   fr: Stralsund
                                            Gesangbuch
CALL TO PRAYER   Pastoral Prayer
HYMN   "O Worship the King"   Attr.: Haydn
         (Children may come forward at this time.)
CHILDREN'S STORY
WORDS OF WELCOME
SCRIPTURE READING   Job 38
THE MORNING OFFERING
   Anthem   "Song of Exaltation"   Beck
                           Choir
   Doxology
   Prayer of Dedication

SERMON   "The Lords' Presence—At the End of your Rope"

Tramping the troubled topography of Job one finds pain on every page. There is also a message from the Lord here—a word of comfort and consolation. Here our humanity is laid bare, but there is more, a glimpse of God as well.

Job was a good man, "blameless and upright"; he "feared God and turned away from evil" (1:1). He suffered a series of dreadful losses: his wealth, his family, and finally, his health. Still, Job kept his faith. Job's friends came to comfort but became a part of his affliction. They shouted advice from safe ground. They tried to make Job's case fit their Procrustean theology: "You are suffering terribly. Obviously, you are a sinner, or you would not be suffering so. Confess your sins."

Job never contended he was not a sinner, but he had done nothing to deserve his awful suffering. Job complained bitterly, pleaded, and longed for vindication. Job suffered more than a man can stand.

Then, to the wonder of all, God answered. He did not answer Job's "why?" But he answered Job. Heaven heard his plea. God answered Job from a storm or whirlwind. A tornado had killed his children. In the thunder and dark clouds there was a theophany, an appearance of God. The Lord is not simply a storm Deity, for He also stills the storms—as on Galilee.

God revealed that He is at work in the universe, the world of nature. He is aware of the forces of evil (symbolized by behemoth and leviathan). God cared and came to Job. Many people claim they believe in God but lack a personal relationship with Him. The universe is so vast they wonder how God could be concerned about one person. They are like the child who misquoted the Lord's Prayer, "Our Father, who art in heaven, how do You know my name?" God is real and personal. The incarnation demonstrated that.

In Job 38—39, we have an epic poem about the world of nature. God is shown to be Creator of the earth, the sea, and time. The natural order is celebrated: snow, hail, lightning, clouds, and the starry constellations. Animals are described, including the lion, mountain goats, the wild ass and wild ox, the ostrich and eagle, the war-horse, hippo (behemoth), and crocodile (leviathan). The passage recalls the hymn: "All things bright and beautiful,/All things great and small,/All things wise and wonderful;/Our Father made them all."

Job did not find God in his good works or in correct beliefs. He did not discover the Lord in his friends' counsel or even in his suffering. It made Job bitter. Job found the Lord in the midst of his need. L. D. Johnson observed, "Job found God at the end of his rope," at his extremity. There Job accepted his own humanity and trusted God. "I need Thee, O I need Thee;/Ev'ry hour I need Thee!"

In God's answer, Job learned the limits of his own knowledge and strength. He felt small and fell silent, "I lay my hand on my mouth" (40:4).

Job gained a firsthand experience of the Lord. He no longer knew him only by hearsay. Job asked for vindication, but he received better than he asked. Job experienced God for himself: "I had heard of thee by the hearing of the ear,/but now my eye sees thee" (42:5).

Job repented. His arrogance turned to adoration. His demands gave way to silence. His sense of self-importance turned to the perspective of an obedient child of God. Job accepted the limitations of his own humanity and learned to place his trust in God.

We can learn some lessons from this study of Job:

• Suffering is not always due to sin.

• Suffering is often a mystery for which we have no adequate explanation.

• It reminds us of our finitude and our dependence on God.

• We learn that the real answer is a clearer view of God.

Job found God present at the end of his rope—and so may we.

> Not until the loom is silent, and the shuttles cease to fly,
> Will God unroll the canvas, and explain the reason why;
> How the dark threads are as needful in the weaver's skilful hand,
> As the threads of gold and silver in the pattern he has planned."[12]

OBSERVANCE OF THE LORD'S SUPPER

   Giving of the Bread

      Solo   "How Great Thou Art"   Arr. Hine

   Giving of the Cup

      Anthem   "Author of Life Divine"   Young

                      Choir

HYMN   "O Love That Wilt Not Let Me Go"   Peace

SHARING OF DECISIONS   Benediction

MOMENT OF SILENCE   Organ Dismissal

16
In Our Worship

PRELUDE	Sanctus	Gounod
HYMN	"I Am Thine, O Lord"	
WELCOME & PRAYER		Doane
HYMN	"Jesus, Thy Boundless Love To Me"	Hemy
THE EVENING OFFERING		
Anthem	"In the Year that King Uzziah Died"	Williams
	Choir	
Offertory Prayer		

SERMON   "The Lord's Presence—In Our Worship"

"In the year that King Uzziah died I saw the Lord sitting upon a throne, high and lifted up; and his train filled the temple. Above him stood the seraphim; each had six wings: with two he covered his face, and with two he covered his feet, and with two he flew. And one called to another and said: 'Holy, holy, holy is the Lord of hosts; the whole earth is full of his glory.' And the foundations of the thresholds shook at the voice of him who called, and the house was filled with smoke. And I said: 'Woe is me! For I am lost; for I am a man of unclean lips, and I dwell in the midst of a people of unclean lips; for my eyes have seen the King, the Lord of hosts!'

"Then flew one of the seraphim to me, having in his hand a burning coal which he had taken with tongs from the altar. And he touched my mouth, and said: 'Behold, this has touched your lips; your guilt is taken away, and your sin forgiven.' And I heard the voice of the

Lord saying, 'Whom shall I send, and who will go for us?' Then I said, 'Here I am! Send me' " (Isa. 6:1-8).

God comes to us in worship. Isaiah's friend, King Uzziah, had died. Then the young courtier had a vision of the King of kings. It occurred as he was at worship in the Temple. Note his response:

"Woe is me! . . . for I am a man of unclean lips" (v. 5). When we approach Holy God, we know ourselves to be sinners. An angelic figure touched Isaiah's lips with a live coal from the altar and said, "Your guilt is taken away, and your sin forgiven" (v. 7). Next, the voice of the Lord asked, "Whom shall I send, and who will go for us?" Isaiah responded, "Here I am! Send me" (V. 8).

Isaiah found God present within his worship in the Temple. The two from Emmaus knew the Lord was real to them at their dinner table. They realized their guest was none other than the risen Christ when He broke bread in their home. Who can forget their spiritual "heartburn" at being in the presence of the Lord?

Saul encountered the risen Christ on the road while traveling to Damascus. His response was much like Isaiah's: "Lord, what will you have me do?"

We may meet the Lord in our worship: in the place of worship, in our homes, or on the road. Worship is both corporate and private.

Worship's function is twofold: to comfort us and to confront us with the claims of the gospel and the Christian ethic. Therefore, preaching is both priestly and prophetic.

Worship means to ascribe supreme worth to God. Our word comes from an old Anglo-Saxon root, "worth-ship." Worship is is our offering to God (Rom. 12:1-2).

Read in unison William Temple's definition of worship:

"Worship is the submission of all our nature to God. It is the quickening of conscience by His holiness; the nourishment of the mind with His truth; the purifying of imagination by His beauty; the opening of the heart to His love; the surrender of will to His purpose— and all of this gathered up in adoration, the most selfless emotion of which our nature is capable and therefore the chief remedy for that self-centeredness which is our original sin and the source of all actual sin."[13]

The observance of the Lord's Supper can be a supreme act of worship. Here at the Lord's table the divine Presence may well shine through. This is an opportunity for human-divine encounter. Let us come to the table in bright anticipation.

THE LORD'S SUPPER
  The Bread
    Anthem   "Alas, and Did My Savior Bleed"   Harris
  The Cup
    Duet   "Lovely Appear"   Gounod
         (from "The Redemption")
HYMN   "Blest Be the Tie"   Mason

17
In His World

SACRED ORGAN MUSIC   "Jesus, Lover of My Soul"   Hustad
CHIMING OF THE HOUR
INVOCATION AND THE LORD'S PRAYER
HYMN OF CONSECRATION   "Guide Me, O Thou Great Jehovah"
                                      Hughes
WORDS OF WELCOME
HYMN OF PRAISE   "How Great Thou Art"
SCRIPTURE READING
CALL TO PRAYER   Pastoral Prayer
THE MORNING OFFERING
  ANTHEM   "My Eternal King"   Marshall
My God, I love thee; not because I hope for heaven thereby, nor yet because who love Thee not must die eternally. Thou, O my Jesus,

Thou didst me upon the cross embrace; for me didst bear the nails and spear, and manifold disgrace. Why, then why, O blessed Jesus Christ, should I not love Thee well? Not for the hope of winning heaven, or of escaping hell; not with the hope of gaining aught, not seeking a reward; but as Thyself has loved me, O ever loving Lord! E'en so I love Thee, and will love, and in Thy praise will sing; solely because Thou are my God, and my Eternal King![14]

DOXOLOGY
PRAYER OF DEDICATION

SERMON   "The Lord's Presence—In His World"

"In the beginning God created the heavens and the earth. The earth was without form and void, and darkness was upon the face of the deep; and the Spirit of God was moving over the face of the waters.

"And God said, 'Let there be light'; and there was light.' " (Gen. 1:1-3).

"Then God said, 'Let us make man in our image, after our likeness; and let them have dominion over the fish of the sea, and over the birds of the air, and over the cattle, and over all the earth, and over every creeping thing that creeps upon the earth.' So God created man in his own image, in the image of God he created him; male and female he created them" (Gen. 1:26-27)

"And God saw everything that he had made, and behold, it was very good. And there was evening and there was morning, a sixth day" (Gen. 1:31).

"Have this mind among yourselves, which is yours in Christ Jesus, who, though he was in the form of God, did not count equality with God a thing to be grasped, but emptied himself, taking the form of a servant, being born in the likeness of men. And being found in human form he humbled himself and became obedient unto death, even death on a cross. Therefore God has highly exalted him and bestowed on him the name which is above every name, that at the name of Jesus every knee should bow, in heaven and on earth and under the earth, and every tongue confess that Jesus Christ is Lord, to the glory of God the Father" (Phil. 2:5-11).

Christianity has been accused of being too "other-worldly." Some chide Christians for being so heavenly minded that we are no earthly good. But that is simply not so! The Christian faith is appropriately concerned about humanity's welfare on earth as in heaven. The church has been the mother of colleges and hospitals, as well as institutions for the care of children, the aged and retarded. William Temple considered Christianity the most "materialistic" of all world religions. We believe that God made the world, and He is present in it. Jesus reminded His disciples then and now, "Truly, I say to you, as you did it to one of the least of these my brethren, you did it to me" (Matt. 25:40).

The Creation . . .

. . . is not here by chance but due to the activity of a personal divine Being. *Pantheism* means that "all is God," the natural world is God. "Mother Nature" is God. Pantheism is incorrect, for it equates God with creation. It would limit God, making him a prisoner of His own creation. The natural world is impersonal, but the God who made it is a Person.

Deism would remove God from the world of nature. This view sees Him as detached from creation. God would be like a cosmic clockmaker who made the world and set it running. However, afterward He would be uninvolved, leaving the world to operate according to natural law. Thomas Jefferson was a Deist.

Theism is a third view of the relationship between the Creator and His creation. It holds that God is both involved with and beyond the natural world. He is both immanent (with us) and transcendent (beyond us). The Lord is in the world, and He is above the world. God and nature are not the same. He is neither imprisoned in the world He has made, nor is He divorced from it.

Creation's function is both to provide for us and to point us to its Maker. Archibald Rutledge wrote about a woman who went to visit in a mountain cabin at word of her neighbor's death. The room was fairly dark and smelled of hickory ashes in the fireplace. On the mantle, there was a large rhododendron blossom. She remarked on the beauty of the flower. The widow replied, "Yes, it 'minds me of God." Nature's purpose is to remind us of God—the Creator.

The Incarnation . . .

. . . is an indication that God has come into His world. At the advent or birth of Jesus, God became flesh and literally entered history.

In ancient times the Lord made covenants. They were agreements initiated by God. These relationships contained great promises and were conditioned on human obedience. The Lord made covenant promises to Adam, Abraham, Israel, and King David. The prophet Isaiah foresaw a day when God would make a new covenant with humanity. It would be written in human hearts, not on tablets of stone. The new covenant would be inward and not simply external. At the first observance of the Lord's Supper, Jesus said, "This cup is the new covenant in my blood" (1 Cor. 11:25).

Jesus' name was Immanuel, which means God is present *with us* here on earth. "*In Christ* God was reconciling the world to himself" (2 Cor. 5:19). The cosmic Christ, the eternal Word of God, emptied Himself and became fully obedient to the Father. Jesus was man as God meant for him to be.

Our Worship . . .

. . . is the place and time where we are most likely to encounter God in His world. In the Lord's Supper, we have signs of His Presence. They are not magical or mechanical means of grace, but they are significant symbols which remind us of His sacrifice on our behalf. We can become aware that He is with us as we worship Him. "Christ in you, the hope of glory" (Col. 1:27).

We come to have fellowship with one another and to meet the Lord at the table. Those who are ill and hurt come for healing. The brokenhearted come for comfort. The guilty can confess their sins and find forgiveness here. Those who are discouraged can have their faith strengthened.

In communion we come to Christ, but He also comes to us. These are the gifts of God for the people of God. Albert Schweitzer, missionary to Africa, wrote, "He comes to us as one unknown . . . as of old by the lakeside, he came to those men who knew him not. He speaks to us the same words, 'Follow thou me' and sets us to the tasks he has to fulfill in our time. He commands and to those who obey . . . He will reveal himself . . . and they shall learn in their own experience who he is."[15]

Gerhard Claas, general secretary of the Baptist World Alliance, led a communion service for a Russian Baptist Church. The Soviet pastor said, "We are celebrating the Lord's Supper. We are not looking for philosophy or high words. We desire only one thing: to see Jesus."

At the Lord's table we would see Jesus and celebrate His presence with us—here in this world.

OBSERVANCE OF THE LORD'S SUPPER
  Giving of the Bread
    Solo   "They Could Not"   Harris-Cloninger
  Giving of the Cup
    Anthem   "Near to the Heart of God"   Lyall
                      Choir
HYMN OF INVITATION   Allen
    "Must Jesus Bear the Cross Alone?"
SHARING OF DECISIONS   Benediction
MOMENT OF SILENCE   Organ Dismissal

18
In His Word

SACRED ORGAN MUSIC   "If Thou But Suffer God to Guide Thee"
                                     Bach

INVOCATION AND THE LORD'S PRAYER
HYMN OF GOD'S WORD "O Word of God Incarnate" Mendelssohn
WORDS OF WELCOME
HYMN OF GOD'S WORD "Word of God Across the Ages" Haydn
SCRIPTURE READING   Jeremiah 36:17-24
CALL TO PRAYER   Pastoral Prayer
THE MORNING OFFERING

   Anthem   "Thy Word Is a Light"   Morgan
                           Choir

   Doxology
   Prayer of Dedication

SERMON   "The Lord's Presence—In His Word"

"Then they asked Baruch, 'Tell us, how did you write all these words? Was it at his dictation?' Baruch answered them, 'He dictated all these words to me, while I wrote them with ink on the scroll.' Then the princes said to Baruch, 'Go and hide, you and Jeremiah, and let no one know where you are.'

"So they went into the court to the king, having put the scroll in the chamber of Elishama the secretary; and they reported all the words to the king. Then the king sent Jehudi to get the scroll, and he took it from the chamber of Elishama the secretary; and Jehudi read it to the king and all the princes who stood beside the king. It was the ninth month, and the king was sitting in the winter house and there was a fire burning in the brazier before him. As Jehudi read three or four columns, the king would cut them off with a penknife and throw them into the fire in the brazier, until the entire scroll was consumed in the fire that was in the brazier. Yet neither the king, nor any of his servants who heard all these words, was afraid, nor did they rend their garments." (Jer. 36:17-24).

"In the beginning was the Word, and the Word was with God, and the Word was God. He was in the beginning with God." (John 1:1).

The English poet John Masefield wrote *The Widow in the Bye Street*. It tells about a brokenhearted mother in a London slum who watched the police take her only son to be hanged for stealing. She cried out, "Life is just a lot of broken things, too broke to mend!" The reality of her statement is enough to make an optimist shiver.

There are *broken dreams*. "For of all words of tongue or pen,/The saddest are these: 'It might have been.' "

We see many *broken families*. A newspaper article was entitled "My Best Christmas." In it a teenager was quoted as saying, "Last Christmas was the best. You see, it was our last one together as a family."

There are *broken spirits*. Many suffer beneath the cruel, grinding heel of tyranny. Witness Poland. Many have been disappointed so often and for so long that they have given up in despair.

Where on earth is God? Is He present in His world any longer? Is there any word from the Lord? Yes. God is present in His Word.

God is present in His *prophetic Word*. In the sixth century BC, "word from the Lord" came to His prophet Jeremiah. It kept coming to him across forty-two years. His prophecy was no fading spark from the campfire. It was a lifelong beacon.

Jeremiah dared declare the unwelcome word from God. As a result he was almost never invited to dinner a second time! Yet the eternal Word was present in and speaking through the prophetic words of Jeremiah.

God is present in His *written Word,* the Scriptures. Jeremiah dictated his prophecy and had it transcribed. This message was read to the king in his winter house. With utter disregard for the prophecy, the king cut the scroll and burned it. He was the first "Bible burner" but unfortunately not the last.

Jeremiah simply redictated his prophecy. We can read it in our Bibles 2,500 years later. The written Word comes alive to us even today. It is both a *window* to show us the Father and a *mirror* in which we see ourselves, in both our need and our worth.

God was present in the *Living Word,* the incarnate Christ. We know Jesus through study of the Scriptures and the witness of the Holy Spirit. Most often, we encounter Him in the preaching of the Word.

Jesus is the personal Word of God: "In the beginning was the Word, and the Word was with God, and the Word was God" (John 1:1).

God is present with us in His word: prophetic, written, and personal. We are not alone. This is the good news! Our brokenness can be mended as surely as we assimilate this broken bread into our body tissues. In the words of John Calvin's will, we are "servants of the Word."

Now let us be aware of the divine presence as we gather at the Lord's table to observe the ordinance of the Lord's Supper. Here the written Word of God can come alive to us as we worship the risen Christ—the living Word.

OBSERVANCE OF THE LORD'S SUPPER
  Giving of the Bread
    Solo   "Break Thou the Bread of Life"   Sherwin
  Giving of the Cup
    Chorale   "O Sacred Head, Now Wounded"   Bach
                  Choir
HYMN OF INVITATION   Mason
            "When I Survey the Wondrous Cross"
SHARING OF DECISIONS   Benediction
MOMENT OF SILENCE   Organ Dismissal

19
In Our Fellowship

PRELUDE
HYMN   "Down at the Cross"   Stockton
WELCOME AND PRAYER
THE EVENING OFFERING
  Offertory
  Offertory Prayer

Hymn Medley—one stanza each   B Flat
Hymn   "The Old Rugged Cross"   Bennard
Hymn   "Rock of Ages, Cleft for Me"   Hastings

Sermon   "The Lord's Presence—In Our Fellowship

"The cup of blessing which we bless, is it not a participation in the blood of Christ? The bread which we break, is it not a participation in the body of Christ?" (1 Cor. 10:16).

We might come to church, see the table set for observance of the Lord's Supper, and think or say, "There will be no preaching today!" Don't you believe it. The observance of the ordinance can be one of the most powerful forms of preaching. Indeed, it can be preaching at its best, involving the congregation and using the spoken Word, music, and vivid elements to proclaim eternal truth. Note 1 Corinthians 11:26: "For as often as you eat this bread and drink the cup, you proclaim [show forth, declare] the Lord's death until he comes." Thus, the ordinance is a powerful means of Christian proclamation. I have a friend who led his son to faith in Christ by discussing the meaning of the Lord's Supper.

In addition to its being a form of preaching, the Supper is also a symbol of fellowship. Our text reminds us that the cup is the communion of the blood of Christ and the bread is the communion of the body of Christ. We Baptists tend to shy away from the word *communion,* but the apostle Paul didn't. It is a powerful word. The Greek is that familiar word *koinonia* which means fellowship with, participation in, or sharing. Here it means sharing in the effect of His broken body and shed blood which resulted in our salvation.

Jesus gave His blood, His life for our redemption, that we might be heirs to and enjoy eternal life. "The blood of Jesus Christ his Son cleanseth us from all sin" (1 John 1:7b, KJV). Jesus' body was sacrificed once for all on the cross that death might be forever defeated. In Christ, we are members of His body. Indeed the church is identified as the body of Christ. In that body, there is oneness and unity:

"Because there is one bread, we who are many are one body, for we all partake of the one bread" (1 Cor. 10:17). We who are many are one in Christ. In Ephesians, Paul underlined our oneness in fellowship when he wrote: "There is one body and one Spirit, just as you were called to the one hope that belongs to your call, one Lord, one faith, one baptism, one God and Father of us all, who is above all and through all and in all" (4:4-6).

There is something special about eating together. Table fellowship creates close and meaningful relationships. An Englishman will invite friends to "come for tea." A man of the world will invite another to "have a drink." Business and professional men get together for lunch with clients and with one another in luncheon clubs. Courting couples go out to dinner together. We entertain friends in our homes at dinner parties. Our closest times together as a family are often those around the table. At our home we've found this a splendid time for sharing family concerns. Yes, there is something special about eating together, something highly symbolic." We need to remember that Christ is Lord of the dinner table as well as Lord of the communion table.

Notice the prominent place that eating and table fellowship occupies in the Gospel accounts. Some of Jesus' most memorable teaching was done around a table or at a meal. Recall His feeding of the multitudes, His attending banquets, and His appearance to the two at Emmaus. Indeed, the risen Christ said by way of invitation: "Behold, I stand at the door and knock; if any one hears my voice and opens the door, I will come in to him and eat with him, and he with me" (Rev. 3:20). When we eat together, we share at a deep level. This is equally true of our fellowship with the Lord. Actually, heaven contains a banquet hall where we'll eat together in the presence of God. Imagine! Sitting at table, eating with God! Surely, the Lord's Supper offers us a glimpse of what it will be like to sit at the Lamb's table in glory.

The Lord's Supper is such an opportunity for table fellowship (sharing and communion). John wrote, "Truly our fellowship is with the father, and with his Son Jesus Christ" (1 John 1:3b, KJV). Christ is the head of the family, and we are family members. He is host at the Lord's table, and we are His guests, sharing in fellowship with Him.

More than this vertical fellowship in the presence of Christ and the Father, there is also a horizonal fellowship at the Lord's table. We eat together with other believers. They are our brothers and sisters in Christ. Here is the truest fraternity—around the table of our Lord. By our baptism we were united with the body of Christ. By periodically sharing at the Lord's table, we renew our companionship and strengthen our union and oneness with Him and with each other. This is the observance, the symbol, which unites the church. Just as we were united with the church in our baptism, so our relationship is cemented and renewed at the Lord's table.

As we come to the table together, let us hear the reading of our (First Baptist Church, Greensboro, North Carolina) church covenant and be reminded of our common bonds:

As we trust we have been brought by divine grace to embrace the Lord Jesus Christ, and by the influence of His spirit to give up ourselves wholly to Him, so we do now solemnly covenant with each other that, God helping us, we will walk together in Him in brotherly love.

That, as members one of another for the glory of Christ in the salvation of men, we will exercise a Christian care and watchfulness over each other, and as occasion may require, faithfully warn, rebuke and admonish one another in the spirit of meekness, considering ourselves lest we also be tempted.

That we will willingly submit to, and conscientiously enforce, all wholesome discipline of the church;

That we will uphold the worship of God and the ordinances of His house by regular attendance thereon, search diligently the Scriptures, observe closet or family worship, and seek to train up those under our care to the glory of God in the salvation of their souls;

That, as we have been planted together in the likeness of His death by baptism, and raised from an emblematic grace in newness of life, especially will we seek divine aid to enable us to walk circumspectly and watchfully in the world, denying all ungodliness and every worldly lust;

That we will remember the poor, and contribute cheerfully of our means for their relief, and for the maintenance of a faithful gospel ministry among us, and for the spread of the same to the ends of the earth;

That we will endeavor, by example and effort, to win souls to Christ; and,
Through life, amidst evil report and good report, seek to live to the praise of Him who hath called us out of darkness into His marvelous light to whom be glory and honor and power for ever and ever, Amen.

Let us approach the table for this observance. It is a symbol of our fellowship, with the risen Christ and with one another. Let us break bread, together. We will drink the cup, together. We will find Christ present and real to us in this Supper; and we will find each other precious. May this *koinonia* meal bind us to Christ and to each other, as we both remember and proclaim His death.

OBSERVANCE OF THE LORD'S SUPPER
    Giving of the Bread
        Piano Meditation   "The Bond of Love"   Skillings
    Giving of the Cup
        Solo   "They'll Know We Are Christians by Our Love"
                                                  Scholtes
HYMN   "Blest Be the Tie"   Mason

20
And Our Unity

PREPARATION FOR WORSHIP
SACRED ORGAN MUSIC   "Be Thou My Vision"   Thiman
OPENING SENTENCES
    Leader: Christ brings us together in His love and unifies us by His call to be His people.
    People: Because He loves us all, we love each other.
    Leader: Thus we gather as a community of faith, the church of Jesus Christ, the family of God.
    People: We give thanks to God for reconciling us to Himself and

to each other, and take on ourselves the ministry of
reconciliation.

HYMN OF UNITY   "We Are Called to Be God's People"   Haydn
WORDS OF WELCOME
HYMN OF UNITY   "Forward Through the Ages"   Sullivan
SCRIPTURE READING   1 Corinthians 10:16-17
                              1 Corinthians 11:20-22

CALL TO PRAYER
PASTORAL PRAYER
THE MORNING OFFERING
    Anthem   "Heavenly Father"   Schubert/Thompson
                              Sanctuary Choir
CONGREGATIONAL RESPONSE   Schumann
    Bless Thou the gifts our hands have brought;
    Bless Thou the work our hearts have planned;
    Ours is the faith, the will, the thought,
    The rest, O God, is in Thy hand. Amen.
PRAYER OF DEDICATION

SERMON   "The Lord's Presence—And Our Worth"
                 1 Corinthians 10:16-17; 11:20-29

Americans are a diverse people. There is probably no other nation
which contains citizens of so many different national and ethical
origins. We have been called a "melting pot," but there are still a lot
of lumps! We are like a bowl of chili in which most of the ingredients
can still be identified.

The people in our denomination, too, are diverse in many ways. We
reach across the socioeconomic spectrum. We don't even agree on all
the fine points of our theological beliefs, yet we are one in our loyalty
to Jesus Christ and His Great Commission. A "Peanuts" cartoon
showed various characters looking at a cloud formation and identify-
ing what they saw. Lucy imagined the bust of Rembrandt. Linus
thought he saw the map of Nova Scotia. Charlie Brown said, "I was
gonna say I saw a horsey and a ducky."

The Lord's Supper is a symbol of our unity as members of the family of God. It represents the stack pole of our faith which ever calls us back to the basics of the gospel and our salvation.

The earliest account of the institution of the Lord's Supper in the Bible is found in 1 Corinthians. This writing predates that of the Gospels. Look at 1 Corinthians 10:16: "The cup of blessing which we bless, is it not the communion of the blood of Christ? The bread which we break, is it not the communion of the body of Christ?" (KJV). What does this mean? Surely there is more mystery here than we can grasp or explain.

Communion means "participation in" (RSV) the life and death of Christ. We are His beneficiaries, His gospel heirs. Communion also means "fellowship with." It is like participation in and having fellowship at a special family meal. Christ is our Host as well as our Shepherd. Communion is a shared experience in worship at the Lord's Table. My denomination may be hesitant to use the word *communion*, but the apostle Paul had no such reluctance.

The Lord's Supper is a sign of our unity, our oneness in Christ. "We are all partakers of that one bread" (1 Cor. 10:17). We are one. Communion unites us with Christ and with each other.

People tend to be class conscious today, as they did in the first century. Many barriers separate us: social and economic, educational and sexual barriers. The church is the one place in society where the barriers are down, where these artificial distinctions are meaningless, where we are in fact one—in Christ.

The one loaf and one cup symbolize that the church is one body. Edwin Markham wrote:

> He drew a circle that shut me out—
> Heretic, rebel, a thing to flout.
> But Love and I had the wit to win:
> We drew a circle that took him in."

We are the family, the household of God: "One Lord, one faith, one baptism." We are united beneath the lordship of Christ.

Our observance of communion is double edged:

It is fellowship with the risen Christ who is present with us.

And it is fellowship with other believers.
Let us join hands and quietly sing,

We are one in the Spirit;
We are one in the Lord.

OBSERVANCE OF THE LORD'S SUPPER
  Giving of the Bread
                    "Call to Remembrance"   Farrant
                          Ensemble
  Giving of the Cup
                  "O Sacred Head, Now Wounded"   Bach
                            Choir

HYMN OF INVITATION
                    "Blest Be the Tie"   Mason
SHARING OF DECISIONS   Benediction
MOMENT OF SILENCE   Organ Dismissal

21
In the Communion of the Saints

PRELUDE   "Theme and Variants"   Zabel
                         Handbell Choir
CALL TO PRAISE   "Sing unto the Lord a New Song"   Young
                            Psalm 96
                              Choir
RESPONSIVE CALL TO WORSHIP   Psalm 9
   Leader: I will give thanks to the Lord with my whole heart;
   All: I will tell of all Thy wonderful deeds.
   Leader: I will be glad and exult in Thee;
   All: I will sing praise to Thy name, O Most High.

Leader: The Lord is a stronghold for the oppressed, a stronghold in times of trouble.

All: And those who know Thy name put their trust in Thee, for Thou, O Lord, hast not forsaken those who seek Thee.

Leader: Sing praises to the Lord, who dwells in Zion! Tell among the peoples His deeds!

Hymn   From "Stralsund Gesangbuch"
"Praise to the Lord, the Almighty"

Ordinance of Baptism

Words of Welcome

Hymn   "Joyful, Joyful, We Adore Thee"   Beethoven

The Morning Offering

   Offertory   "Toccata in A Minor"   McCleary
Youth Handbell Choir

   Congregational Response

All things are Thine: no gift have we, /Lord of all gifts, to offer Thee,/
And hence with grateful hearts today/
Thine own before Thy feet we lay. Amen.

   Prayer of Dedication

Scripture Reading Hebrews 11:1-2, 12:1-2

Call to Prayer   Pastoral Prayer

Sermon

"The Lord's Presence—in the Communion of the Saints"

"Let us draw near with a true heart in full assurance of faith, with our hearts sprinkled clean from an evil conscience and our bodies washed with pure water. Let us hold fast the confession of our hope without wavering, for he who promised is faithful." (Heb. 10:22-23).

"Therefore, since we are surrounded by so great a cloud of witnesses, let us also lay aside every weight, and sin which clings so closely, and let us run with perseverance the race that is set before us, looking to Jesus the pioneer and perfecter of our faith, who for the joy that was set before him endured the cross, despising the shame, and is seated at the right hand of the throne of God." (Heb. 12:1-2).

Jesus was a country man. He grew up in a small town, little more than a village. Nazareth is perched on a mountain range, overlooking the vast Plain of Esdraelon. When Jesus came to preach and teach, He drew His illustrations from that rural village setting.

He talked about sparrows twittering on the ground, about sowing grain in the plowed field, about making bread. As a child, did you ever watch your mother or grandmother make bread?

Jesus spoke about losing a coin and turning the house upside down to recover it, about a shepherd who had a hundred sheep, lost one, and left the ninety-nine to go after the one that was lost. His illustrations were drawn from country and village life, and they are true to life today.

The apostle Paul was a urban man in contrast to Jesus. He was born and grew up in a major city, Tarsus, in Asia Minor. He was educated at the University of Jerusalem under the most famous teacher there, Gamaliel. When Paul wrote and preached, he drew his illustrations from a totally different culture and context than did Jesus.

Paul illustrated spiritual truths by writing about the law courts, about sailing, or by describing a Roman soldier's armor. He drew numerous illustrations from the world of athletics, the Greco-Roman stadium and games. Paul's word pictures were vastly different but equally meaningful.

The passage I read from Hebrews obviously draws on the imagery of the Greek games. Paul used the Greek athletic stadium to illustrate a precious Christian doctrine, the communion of the saints. It is one we would do well to look at on this Memorial Day communion service.

Who are the saints? They are not a New Orleans ball team. For the first 300 years in the history of the Christian church, Christianity was an illegal religion. It went underground. Christians were hunted down and persecuted. Many were martyred, including most of the twelve apostles. Paul himself was beheaded outside the city of Rome, according to tradition.

Christians worshiping in Rome had to meet in a clandestine fashion. South of the city of Rome they began to dig a tunnel system in the lava rock which makes up the subsoil there. In little cubicles dug back in the side of the corridor, they would bury their dead. Many of those dead were martyrs, believers who had been killed for their faith.

Christians met before daylight underground to worship and sing their songs of faith. They read the Holy Scriptures and recited their sermons in semidarkness. The altar for the communion service might have been on the tomb of one of those martyrs.

Not long after the turn of the fourth century, something happened in the Roman world. Emperor Constantine was converted. When he became a Christian, he made Christianity the established religion of the Roman Empire. Christians could literally come out from underground; They could gather and worship in public; they could witness openly and win others to faith in Christ.

They removed the bones of those martyrs out of the catacombs—most of those graves are empty today. When they built a new church, they would place some of these relics, some of the bones of the saints, underneath the altar. In the Middle Ages, the relics of the saints came to be revered. Those bones became worth more than gold.

In Christian history we called those early martyrs "saints." However, that is not the New Testament meaning of the word *saints.* The definition of the New Testament word for saint means "holy" or "dedicated to God" (*hagios*). By definition a New Testament saint is one who believes in and follows Jesus.

All born-again Christians are "called to be saints," to live a holy life dedicated to God. According to the New Testament, every believer is called to a holy life and a God-pleasing life. Every Christian is called to be a saint.

A saint may be defined as someone who experiences the joy of a remarkable discovery: God's love and God's grace. A saint is one who has the joy of a vast deliverance, deliverance from the power and tyranny of sin. A saint is one who experiences the joy of a single-hearted purpose, committing one's life to do the will of God. You and I are called to be saints, to believe in Jesus and follow Him.

Well, if that's who the saints are, what do we mean by the communion of the saints? The Greek word for communion is *koinonía* which means partnership or fellowship with. It was a common word in Paul's day. In the Greco-Roman world *koinonía* was used to describe a business relationship of partners or an educational relationship between a professor and his students. The word was used commonly to describe a marriage relationship, the communion of husband and wife. Members of a clan also enjoyed *koinonía* or fellowship.

The New Testament picks up that ordinary *koinonía* and applies it to fellow believers. All the saints, all the believers are called into communion, into fellowship, into partnership with Christ. We are called to share, to meet one another's needs, to worship God, and to share our faith. The communion of the saints is a shared fellowship.

Well, if that's who the saints are—ordinary believers in Christ in communion with one another—then *where* are the saints? There are saints in this congregation. Every Christian is a saint. They are men and women of faith who have a radiance about their life that sets them apart from the crowd. They are persons who tend to be holy and heroic in their faith.

Visiting in the hospital, I mentioned a member of our church who was ill. The patient said, "I dearly love to hear that man pray. He seems to speak with God so naturally and from the heart." The saints here will never be canonized, but we believe the saints pray directly to the Father through Christ. He is our Intercessor. But there are saints in the membership of this church, literally.

There are also saints throughout the world. Wherever we go in the earth, we can find saints of God, men, women, and young people who know and love the Lord Christ. They are our brothers and sisters in the Lord, who share our faith and our common allegiance to Him.

One Sunday morning I attended worship in the city of Ogbomosho, Nigeria, in a Baptist Church. The sermon was in Yoruba; the hymns were in Yoruba; the announcements were in Yoruba. Everything was in a foreign language to me, but when they sang "Amazing Grace," I knew the tune and felt a kinship with beautiful black believers in the Lord Christ. We were spiritual kinsfolk. Despite our different cultures and different tongues, we had a common faith and loyalty to the Lord.

We were fellow, born-again, baptized believers. There are saints throughout the whole wide earth; all believers—rich and poor, learned and untutored, Black and White and Oriental, in capitalist and communist countries—are saints wherever they go. There is a worldwide communion of the saints.

Our text speaks about saints in another setting. It tells of every family in heaven and on earth who hear the Father's name. There are saints in this church and throughout the world. There is also a gigantic host of saints in glory, in heaven. That group is made up of some people whom you and I know well.

My father is there. My grandparents are there. Some of my professors are in the communion of the saints in glory—William Barclay, that marvelous Scot; George Buttrick, insightful preacher; the lady who taught me to love English literature when I was in high school are all on the "other side." You have friends there as well. Our text also tells us that those we have loved and lost for a season are there, watching how we run. "Oh, for the touch of an unseen hand, oh, for the sound of a voice now still."

Not only is the church militant made up of those whom we have known and loved; it is also composed of the heroes of the faith across the ages.

I have worshiped at Mansfield College Chapel at Oxford. The chapel is crammed with statues and stained-glass windows of the great heroes of the faith—the apostles, Moses and Abraham, John Calvin and Martin Luther, Zwingli and Huss, David Livingstone and William Carey are depicted. Women, including Monica (Augustine's mother) and Joan of Arc, are there. A visit there is a vivid lesson in church history. We worship surrounded by those who have gone before us in the faith. They are in glory, and they are watching how we run the race.

William Barclay once commented, "When you think about those who've gone before, it makes you humble." It makes one humble, but it also constitutes a challenge. We dare not be mediocre because we've entered into the communion of the saints. Their watching challenges us to moral grandeur, to give our best because they have gone before us. We must hand the faith on.

The author of Hebrews described them as a "great cloud of witnesses" (Heb. 12:1). Can you imagine that? Surrounding us on all sides, they are a cloud of witnesses in God's grandstand. There they are, tier upon tier, cheering us on. The word for witness in Greek is *martyr*.

The contest we have entered is the race of the Christian life. We run it with certain handicaps. The Scripture says, "We have this treasure in earthen vessels" (2 Cor. 4:7). In another passage the author says, "Let us lay aside every weight, and the sin which doth so easily beset us" (Heb. 12:1, KJV). We are to run with patience the race that is set before us.

The goal of the race: "looking to Jesus" (Heb. 12:2). We don't just run for a finish line; we run toward Christ, looking to Jesus, the pioneer of our faith. Two hundred years ago, the eastern United States was wilderness. Our ancestors came through this area going West. They were pioneering. They would mark the trail so others would follow them. Jesus is our pioneer. He has gone before us as the Pioneer of our faith.

Hebrews says something more. He is also the Perfecter of our faith, the Finisher of our faith. "He who began a good work in you will bring it to completion" (Phil. 1:6). Do you ever have times of doubt and trouble when you say, "Lord, I just don't know what I am going to do"? It is wonderful to know that since He has saved you, you can trust Him to keep you. He will see us through to the end.

The "Recessional," Rudyard Kipling's poem, speaks to us as we think about those who have gone on before us: "God of our fathers, known of old . . ."

May God give us the consolation and encouragement of the communion of the saints.

The Lord's Supper is a reminder that we are not alone. We can be assured of the Lord's presence with us. And we can remember that the saints surround and encourage us in the race of faith.

Come, let us remember Jesus Christ and celebrate His presence in our worship at the table.

OBSERVANCE OF THE LORD'S SUPPER
  Giving of the Bread
  Giving of the Cup
HYMN OF INVITATION   "My Faith Looks Up to Thee"   Mason
SHARING OF DECISION   Benediction
MOMENT OF SILENCE   Organ Dismissal

22
In Our Repentance

PRELUDE
CALL TO WORSHIP
HYMN   "When Morning Gilds the Skies"   Barnby
WORDS OF WELCOME
HYMN   "Strong, Righteous Man of Galilee"   Dykes
CALL TO PRAYER   "Show, O Lord, Thy Blessed Face" Words,
                                              Hendricks
  (Hymn: "Bread of Heaven, on Thee We Feed"; Tune: Holley)
Show, O Lord, Thy Blessed face,/ Comfort give and loving grace./
For the tasks that we should do,/ Light and strength must come from
You./ Speak thru channels of Thy voice,/ And grant us to know Thy
voice,/ Knowing, answer in Thy way;/ Show Thyself, O Lord, we
pray. Amen.[16]
PASTORAL PRAYER
THE MORNING OFFERING
  Anthem   "Great Is the Lord"   Cooper/Angell
                         Choir
  Gloria Patri
  Prayer of Dedication

SERMON   "The Lord's Presence—In Our Repentance"

Psalm 51:1-17

In the Christian calendar late winter/early spring is a season of preparation for the coming of Easter. Many churches spend those weeks in preparation for spring revival services. This is a period for self-examination and the confession of our sins.

Psalm 51, the greatest of the seven "penitential psalms," is read in worship this time of year. It is excellent preparation for our observance of the Lord's Supper.

Eric Routley called Psalm 51 "a mirror of life." It is timeless and has a universally valid message for us. Here is high drama. The psalm teaches about the seriousness of sin, the pain of guilt, and the joy of forgiveness and restoration.

The setting of Psalm 51 is one of royal repentance—a king's pardon from the King of kings. David was a teenage hero after he killed the Philistine giant Goliath. His name was on everyone's mind and lips. A young man of deep integrity, in time David became the warrior king of Israel. Then at the height of his powers he had a sordid affair with another man's young wife, Bathsheba. The husband, Uriah, was sent to his death at the battle front on King David's orders.

After a year of David's bearing his guilt, the prophet of the Lord, Nathan, called at the royal court. Shrewdly, and with considerable courage, Nathan told David a parable and then nailed the king's guilt, saying, "You are the man" (2 Sam. 12:1-7). David's greatness is most clearly seen in his repentance. The king's royal repentance is the backdrop of Psalm 51.

1. "Have Mercy on Me" (vv. 1-2)

Here we see the dark side of human nature clearly depicted.

The psalmist used three different strong words for sin.

• *Sin* is missing the mark. It is that moral failure which does not measure up to God's requirements. When we compare our lives to those of other people, we know we may measure up fairly well. But when we put our lives alongside Christ, we come short (Rom. 3:23).

• *Transgression* is an even stronger term. It describes our deliberate, overt sinning. We rebel against God and do what we know to be wrong. This is sometimes called "sinning with a high hand," openly and purposefully.

• *Iniquity* is an even stronger word for sin and evil. It may be translated "crooked" or "perverse" and may even be "demonic." A portrait artist painted my picture. He posed me beside a curtainless window. Thus, the right side of my face was brightly lighted, while the left side was in shadows. He was showing the two sides of human nature. We are creatures made from the dust, and at the same time we were made in the image and likeness of God. We have a dual nature.

David's plea for pardon was based on the nature of God. "Have mercy on me," he prayed. Mercy comes from the Hebrew word for *womb*. It reflects the mother's tender love for the child of her own body. God's "steadfast love" is His covenant love (*chesed*). God loves as one who is in relationship to us.

2. The Confession of Sin (vv. 3-5)

David spoke candidly about his guilt, "My sin is ever before me." This phrase reminds us of Lady Macbeth trying to wash King Duncan's blood from her guilty hands. Guilt is not all bad. In fact, it can be a vital part of our moral warning system. Guilt is to the spirit what pain is to the body. It creates moral discomfort and alerts us to the fact that something is wrong in our lives and ethics. In Lima, Peru, at the site of an inquisition I saw a tiny cell. It was so small a man could not stand in it or lie down. It was called "Little Ease."

We are sinners from birth—born to sinful parents. Still, David acknowledged that he was responsible for his immoral actions. He spoke about "my sin . . . my transgressions . . . my iniquities." David lamented, "Against thee, thee only, have I sinned" (v. 4). When we do wrong we violate other people and ourselves. But at root, all sin is against God. We break God's law; we break His heart. Seeing the harm we have done calls us to repentance.

3. Forgiveness (vv. 6-9)

What does God expect of us? "Thou desirest truth in the inward being" (v. 6). God simply asks that we do what is right, that we have personal integrity.

Note David's plea for pardon: "Purge me with hyssop, and I shall be clean;/ wash me, and I shall be whiter than snow./ Fill me with joy and gladness" (vv. 7-8).

He called for renewal (vv. 10-12). "Create in me a clean heart, O God,/ and put a new and right spirit within me" (v. 10). The Hebrew word for create is *bara*—and only God creates. We are helpless to deal with our own guilt. We cannot wish it away. We need divine forgiveness. We cannot save ourselves—only God can do that.

David prayed that God would "Cast me not away from thy presence" and that he would "Restore to me the joy of thy salvation" (v. 11).

4. The Psalmist's Vow

First, he promised that he would witness to others about the goodness of God (vv. 13-14): "I will teach transgressors thy ways." By sharing his faith, he fully expected to see other sinners return to God. Repentance and restoration to fellowship with God called for a stewardship of sharing his faith with other guilty sinners.

Second, the poet king promised to praise God (vv. 15-16). His gratitude would overflow in worship and joyful thanksgiving. God accepts our repentance, "a broken and a contrite heart" (v. 17). The good news is we can be restored and forgiven. What amazing grace!

As we wait to receive the bread, let us confess our sins to God.

As we wait to receive the cup, let us rejoice in the assurance of His pardon.

Let us meet at the Lord's Table, for He is here in our midst.

OBSERVANCE OF THE LORD'S SUPPER

Giving of the Bread		
Solo	"O Lord Most Holy"	Franck
Giving of the Cup		
Meditation	"When Jesus Wept" Handbell Choir	Billings/Leonard
HYMN	"Fairest Lord Jesus"	Arr. Willis
SHARING OF DECISIONS		
BENEDICTION	MOMENT OF SILENCE	ORGAN DISMISSAL

23
In Our Redemption

SACRED ORGAN MUSIC   "Fantasy in C Major"   Bach
CHIMING OF THE HOUR
INVOCATION AND THE LORD'S PRAYER
HYMN   "Praise to the Lord, the Almighty"   fr. Stralsund
                                                    Gesangbuch
HYMN FOR LABOR DAY   "O Master Workman of Thy Race"
                                                    Burnap
CALL TO PRAYER   Pastoral Prayer
THE MORNING OFFERING
  Anthem   "God of Grace and God of Glory"   Langston
                        Choir
  Gloria Patri
PRAYER OF DEDICATION

SERMON   "The Lord's Presence—in Our Redemption"

In Wayne E. Ward's book *The Drama of Redemption* (Broadman Press), he presented a panoramic view of God's redemptive purpose in the Bible. Redemption is a basic theme which runs throughout the Scriptures.

In Genesis 1 and 2, we have a hymn of creation. Following the fall of mankind, we find the first promise of redemption—the woman's heel will one day bruise the serpent's head. This is called the protevangellium or the "pregospel." Even before the very beginning God envisioned our salvation.

The divine redemptive purpose was behind a series of covenants:

- With Abraham. He was promised that through his descendents all people would be blessed. Jesus was a son of Abraham.
- With Israel at Mount Sinai. This collection of slaves became a chosen people and nation of priests through whom humanity would be blessed (Ex. 19:6).
- With King David. He was promised that his descendants would reign forever. Jesus was a Son of David, and He is sovereign in the eternal kingdom of God.

The prophets interpreted God's covenant and redemptive purpose. Hosea found a gospel in personal heartbreak. Amos called for a return to spiritual religion. Isaiah, a royal courtier, encountered God in worship and promised the coming of Messiah in chapter 53. Micah had a passion for justice. Jeremiah predicted exile, and Ezekiel was a spiritual leader during the Exile in Babylon.

Finally, the long-awaited Messiah was born. Remember that the bright events at Bethlehem had their dark side: the massacre of the infants. Only Mary and Joseph's fleeing to Egypt with their child prevented His execution.

The entire Christ-event was at heart a working out of God's redemptive purpose for humanity. In the birth, ministry, death, and resurrection of Jesus, God was present in His world reconciling a wayward race.

The church is a community of redemption. It is made up of those who are regenerate—born again. Jesus promised: "On this rock I will build my church" (Matt. 16:18). It is still under construction twenty centuries later.

The apostles were eyewitnesses to God's redemptive presence in Christ. Peter wrote that believers are "born anew to a living hope through the resurrection of Jesus Christ from the dead" (1 Pet. 1:3). The great theme of Paul was that salvation means being "in Christ." We have been saved from the penalty of sin. We are currently being saved from sin's tyrannical power. One day we will be saved from the very presence of sin and evil.

The Book of Acts tells the exciting story of the early church in action. Redemption of persons became a reality as the faith spread across the Roman Empire. We tend to forget that it was illegal to be a Christian for 300 years—until Emperor Constantine's conversion.

The church has continued to carry out God's redemptive purpose across the ages. Empowered by the Holy Spirit, brave souls have planted the faith on every continent. Today, our own denomination has the largest foreign missions force overseas.

The Lord's Supper celebrates God's presence and His redemptive purpose—in history, in the church, and in our individual lives. The Supper will continue to be celebrated until the Day of the Lord when the kingdoms of this world shall become "the kingdom of our Lord and of his Christ, and he shall reign for ever and ever" (Rev. 11:15). Amen.

OBSERVANCE OF THE LORD'S SUPPER
    Giving of the Bread
        Solo   "Man of Sorrows"   Bliss
    Giving of the Cup
        Anthem   "Ephesians 2:8-10"   Allen
                            Choir
SOLO   "How Lovely Are Thy Dwellings"   Liddle
HYMN   "Lord, Speak to Me, that I May Speak"   Schumann
SHARING OF DECISIONS   Benediction
MOMENT OF SILENCE   Organ Dismissal

24
When We Confess

PRELUDE   "Festival Fanfare"   Frey
                    Handbell Choir
CALL TO PRAISE   "Awake, My Heart"   Marshall
                        Choir

CALL TO WORSHIP

Leader: God is a God of mystery.

All: THE HOLINESS OF GOD IS HIS OWN.

Leader: God is a God of truth.

All: THE WISDOM OF GOD IS PERFECT.

Leader: God is a God of caring.

All: THE LOVE OF GOD DRAWS US THROUGH CHRIST JESUS INTO INTIMATE FELLOWSHIP WITH HIM.

Leader: God, all Holy and all wise,

All: RECEIVE OUR WORSHIP, THE HUMBLE EXPRESSION OF OUR HEARTS' DESIRE, THE JOYOUS AFFIRMATION OF OUR LIFE IN THEE.[17]

CONGREGATIONAL HYMN   Mozart

Jesus, I my cross have taken,/ All to leave and follow Thee;/ Destitute, despised, forsaken,/ Thou, from hence, my all shalt be;/ Perish ev'ry fond ambition,/ All I've sought or hoped or known;/ Yet how rich is my condition:/ God and heav'n are still my own!

Haste thee on from grace to glory,
    Armed by faith, and winged by prayer;
Heaven's eternal day's before thee,
    God's own hand shall guide thee there;
Soon shall close thy earthly mission,
    Swift shall pass thy pilgrim days;
Hope shall change to glad fruition,
    Faith to sight, and prayer to praise.

WORDS OF WELCOME

HYMN OF DEVOTION   "O Jesus, I Have Promised"   Mann

SCRIPTURE READING   CALL TO PRAYER   PASTORAL PRAYER

SERMON HYMN "Spirit of God, Our Comforter"   Dykes

THE MORNING OFFERING

Offertory   "Psalm 96"   McCleary
                              Handbell Choir

Doxology
Prayer of Dedication

SERMON   "The Lord's Presence—When We Confess"

Isaiah 6:5-7; 1 John 1:8-9

God wants to give us good gifts, and He desires to forgive us our sins. The Lord's Prayer includes both petitions: "Give us this day our daily bread;/ And forgive us our debts,/ As we also have forgiven" (Matt. 6:11-12). We need forgiveness as surely as we need food. The hitch is that our pride makes it difficult for us to confess our sins. George Truett noted that the three hardest words to say are, "I have sinned."

We Need to Confess Our Sins.

Primitive people felt guilt and offered sacrifices to atone for their sins—sometimes human sacrifice. Such is still practiced in some animist religions in Africa.

Modern psychology agrees that we need an appropriate opportunity to confess and experience forgiveness. In his splendid book *Whatever Became of Sin?*, Karl Menninger called for a recovery of the concepts of sin, confession, and forgiveness.

Public figures periodically make confessions. Examples in recent history have included Billie Jean King, Edward Kennedy, Wilbur Mills, John Jenrette, and Richard Nixon.

Isaiah is a biblical example of forgiveness. At worship Isaiah had a vision of God as holy. Then he saw himself as a sinner and confessed, "Woe is me! For I am lost" (Isa. 6:5). Next he experienced spiritual cleansing. In his vision, an angel touched a coal from the altar to the prophet's lips and said, "Your guilt is taken away, and your sin forgiven" (v. 7). We, too, need the assurance of divine pardon. It should be as real as the guilt we felt before confession.

We Can Confess and Be Forgiven.

Our sins may be terrible or trivial, but they separate us from God. Recall the sins of the prodigal son and his elder brother in Luke 15.

Glenn Hinson contends that confession is the most seriously neglected dimension of prayer among Protestants. They reacted to the selling of indulgences and an overemphasis on doing penance in order to earn divine favor. Both theology and psychology agree that "confession is good for the soul." It purifies the conscience, defuses guilt, and enables new beginnings. George Fox noted that the light which reveals also heals.

The Steps in Confession . . .

. . . are quite simple. The first is honest self-examination in which we open ourselves up to God. This is part of our spiritual preparation for taking the Lord's Supper. It is futile to try to play games with the Almighty. We must give up self-deception. For example, an alcoholic may think that no one is aware of his problem.

A second step in confession is genuine repentance. It is not enough to be sorry we were caught in wrong. Repentance is "godly sorrow" for our sins. Judas felt remorse after Jesus' crucifixion, but Simon Peter repented. There is a vast difference in the two.

The third step in confession is a determination to make restitution where possible and to avoid sin in the future. We should turn from the opportunity or the occasion which would lead us to do wrong. We not only accept responsibility for our past actions, we determine to act responsibly for what is right in the future. Recall how Joseph rejected Potiphar's wife's efforts at his seduction.

There is exuberant joy in confession and the realization of God's forgiveness. Burdens are lifted. Pretense and deception are gone. We can begin anew with a clear conscience. The dragon of guilt is slain, and we are set free. We receive the assurance of divine pardon, "If we confess our sins, he is faithful and just to forgive us our sins, and to cleanse us from all unrighteousness" (1 John 1:9, KJV). Glenn Hinson paraphrased that text, "If we confess our sins, God sticks by his promise and plays fair, so that he forgives us our sins and cleanses us from every stain."[18]

We can then go on to forgive others. Grudges are gone, resentments are cleared away. We who have been forgiven must love much.

There are two kinds of confession: the confession of our sins and the confession of our faith. We experience both in the Lord's Presence at the communion table.

OBSERVANCE OF THE LORD'S SUPPER
  Giving of the Bread
    Solo   "When I Survey the Wondrous Cross"   Arr. Harris
    Chorale   "All For Jesus"   Stainer
HYMN OF INVITATION   "Search Me, O God"   Hopkins
SHARING OF DECISIONS   Benediction
MOMENT OF SILENCE   Organ Dismissal

25
When We Pray

SACRED ORGAN MUSIC   "Three Joyous Organ Verses"
CHIMING OF THE HOUR
INVOCATION
HYMN OF PRAISE   "All Hail the Power of Jesus' Name"   Holden
GREETING OF OUR WORSHIPERS
SOLO   "Give God, the Father, Praise"   Shutz
SCRIPTURE READING   Ephesians 6:13-20
CALL TO PRAYER
PASTORAL PRAYER
HYMN OF TRUST   "Faith of Our Fathers"   Hemy
THE MORNING OFFERING
  ANTHEM   "The Lord's Prayer"   Gates
  Congregational Response   Schumann
        Bless Thou the gifts our hands have brought;
        Bless Thou the work our hearts have planned;
        Ours is the faith, the will, the thought;
        The rest, O God, is in Thy hand. Amen.
  Offertory Prayer
SOLO   "Thou Wilt Keep Him in Perfect Peace"   Speaks

SERMON   "The Lord's Presence—When We Pray"

Ephesians 6:13-20

This passage treats the Christian's spiritual warfare and the whole armor of God. Look at the belt of integrity, the shoes of peace, the shield of faith, the helmet of salvation, and the sword of the Spirit which is the Word of God. Now we look at a most personal and precious piece of armor in the arsenal: prayer.

It seems that large numbers of clergy and laity have simply given up on praying because they no longer believe prayer works. I believe God still answers His children's mail. The question is: What kind of correspondent are you?

The Poverty of the Prayerless Life

The neglect of prayer is tragic. By it, we miss out on God's resources, and we miss God Himself. Life can be a wilderness or a paradise. Prayer makes the difference. It puts us in touch with God, enables us to see the mystery, the wonder all around us. The world is itself a miracle, and it is full of miracles which most of us never see, John Killinger reminds us. We need to declare a war on spiritual poverty which is precipitated by prayerlessness!

Most of our failures are due to a lack of prayer. We are much too busy trying to bring in the Kingdom by main force and ingenuity. The Kingdom comes when we pray. It is not when we work for Jesus that we are most successful, but when we allow Jesus to work through us.

Once the American evangelist D. L. Moody preached in a church in England. The atmosphere was ice cold, and Moody couldn't melt it. All afternoon, he dreaded the evening service. But as he stood to preach he detected warmth in a single face, and then in others. He arose to the occasion, and there was a tremendous response at the conclusion of the service. What had made the difference in the two services? One crippled woman had spent the afternoon praying for her church. What would happen if five or ten or a thousand prayed? We would shake our city for Christ!

Prayer makes a difference. It is not simply part of the Christian life—it is the very essence of it. Prayer unleashes spiritual energy. It lets loose in our lives the power and presence of God. Prayer, real prayer, also makes us responsible stewards and sensitive, caring persons. Prayer changes others. Jesus tells us to pray for our enemies because it is impossible! When we pray for an enemy, he becomes a brother. When we pray, we love. Dare we try something so radical?

A Pattern for Effective Prayer

If we are to pray effectively, we need to learn and use patterns for prayer. Don't be surprised at this. You can detect it even in the Lord's Prayer. Jesus did not give the disciples the Model Prayer off the top of His head. It reflects the discipline of His own rich prayer life, and there is a clearly discernible pattern to it. The prayer has six petitions. The first three are directed toward God, and the second three concern our needs.

Let our prayers begin with God. We turn on to the Divine Presence. Suppose you had five uninterrupted minutes in which to speak with the Creator. What would you say, and how would you say it? Wouldn't you give that some careful thought? You do have such an opportunity—each day. You see, the purpose of prayer is relationship, not simply answers. God's greatest gift to us in prayer is Himself!

A second purpose of prayer is to let the mind of Christ be formed in you—to discover His will and His perspective. A student's wife arose thirty minutes early each morning to pray. She made a startling discovery, confessing, "The time I spend on my knees each morning is preparation for prayer. The rest of the day becomes the prayer!"

A third facet of prayer is intercession for healing of bodies and relationships. Frank Laubach, the literacy leader, prayed as he read the newspaper, as he ate in a restaurant, and as he rode on public transportation. He would ask God to aid world leaders and strangers whom he saw about him. We soon learn that giving thanks becomes the bedrock of a growing prayer life, and a life of gratitude results.

You may follow a form prayer such as A.C.T.S.—adoration, confession, thanksgiving, and supplication. I like to meditate on the phrases of the Lord's Prayer each day for a week. Keep a notebook or cards with one phrase on each page. Then jot down the words and phrases which come to mind as you pray that petition each day.

We also have a wealth of devotional literature which can enrich our prayer life. Read classic works on prayer. Spend ten weeks reading H. E. Fosdick's *The Meaning of Prayer.* Read D. M. Baillie's classic *Diary of Private Prayer* or William Barclay's books of *Daily Celebration* or Robert Raines's *Creative Brooding.* Read Lloyd Ogilvie's book *Let God Love You,* devotionals based on the Epistle of Philippians.

Develop the discipline of prayer. Throughout the day find moments in which to "center down," as the Quakers say. Pray periodic ten-second prayers, simply lifting your life into the presence of God.

Jesus Is Our Example

He prayed in all kinds of places: at Herod's Temple and in His hometown synagogue, in the desert, on the mountaintop, and in a bobbing fishing boat on the inland lake of Galilee. He prayed on all sorts of occasions: after His baptism, before choosing His disciples, on entering Jerusalem, in lonely retreats and busy marketplaces. Jesus practiced both private and corporate prayer. He prayed with His disciples and for His disciples, and He taught His disciples to pray. He also asked them to pray with Him, in Gethsemane. He came out of the agony and prayer of Gethsemane "well content," ready for the worst that men and Satan could do to Him. Three of His "seven last words" from the cross were prayers. Jesus knew the rhythm of prayer. If the Son of God needed to speak with the Father so, how much more do we!

God *always* answers our prayers. Sometimes the answer is yes, and at times it is no—but that is an answer nonetheless. Since when does every answer have to be affirmative? There are still other times when the answer is "not yet." God's answer to our prayers is not always what we expect. This is vividly seen in the much-circulated poem by an unknown Confederate soldier:

> I asked God for strength, that I might do greater things,
> I was made weak, that I might learn humbly to obey.
> I asked for health, that I might do greater things,

I was given infirmity, that I might do better things.
I asked for riches, that I might be happy,
I was given poverty, that I might be wise.
I asked for power, that I might have the praise of men,
I was given weakness, that I might feel the need of God.
I asked for all things, that I might enjoy life,
I was given life, that I might enjoy all things.
I got nothing I asked for, but everything I had hoped for.
Almost despite myself, my unspoken prayers were answered,
I am among all men, most richly blessed.

One of the most interesting persons to live in this century was a young German pastor named Dietrich Bonhoeffer. He defied the Nazis and was imprisoned during World War II. In 1945 just at the war's close, he was hanged on the orders of Hitler. An eyewitness to his execution wrote: "Under the scaffold in the sweet spring woods, Bonhoeffer knelt for the last time to pray. Five minutes later, his life was ended."

That Sunday morning, he had been summoned from a worship service he was conducting in the prison to meet the hangman. As Bonhoeffer went out to where the gallows stood, he turned to a friend and said, "For me, this is the end, but also the beginning."

Change that last line above to read: "Five minutes later, his life *began!*"

We are in the Lord's presence when we pray.

ORDINANCE OF THE LORD'S SUPPER
  Giving of the Bread
            "Jesu, Word of God Incarnate"   Mozart
  Giving of the Cup
                "O Sacred Head"   Bach
                    Choir
HYMN OF INVITATION   "Have Thine Own Way, Lord"   Stebbins
THE SHARING OF DECISIONS   Benediction
MOMENT OF SILENCE   Organ Dismissal

26
In Our Faith

SACRED ORGAN MUSIC
              "Christmas Pastorale"   Thiman
LIGHTING OF THE ADVENT WREATH   The Pastor's Family
CAROL   "O Come, All Ye Faithful"   Wade
PRAYER
SOLO   "Love Came Down at Christmas"   Karhu
LITANY

Leader:	There was love here but much of lovelessness,
People:	AND HE CAME.
Leader:	There was truth here but much of error,
People:	AND HE CAME.
Leader:	There was light here but much of obscurity,
People:	AND HE CAME.
Leader:	There was God here but much of inaccessibility,
People:	AND HE CAME.
Leader:	There was sonship here but much of alienation,
People:	AND HE CAME.
Leader:	And because He came,
	Love was rekindled in the ashes of anger;
	Truth surged in error's den;
People:	Light began pushing back the darkness;
	God passed within reach;
All:	And we who were already sons
	received power to become the redeemed sons of God.[19]

DUET   "O Holy Night"   Adam/Hustad
SCRIPTURE READING   Luke 2:1-20
CAROL   "Angels, from the Realms of Glory"   Smart

ATHEM   "Child of Love"   English

SERMON   "The Lord's Presence—In Our Faith"

December 24

Lloyd C. Douglas once asked an elderly music teacher, "What's the good news for today?" At that the teacher struck a tuning fork and replied, "That is *A*. It was *A* yesterday. It will be *A* tomorrow, and it will be *A* a thousand years from now. The piano may be out of tune, and the soprano may be off-key, but that is *A*."

In much the same way, we can declare that the Lord's Supper is *A*. In the midst of the holiday rush, the Supper returns us to the rudiments. In times of war or crisis, the Lord's Supper stands at the center of our faith. It reminds us, in season and out, of God's love and His costly provision of our salvation. In a word, the observance refocuses our faith.

Our Faith Can Become Fragmented

It can be so out of focus that we simply see it in bits and pieces. There have been times in the history of the church when she has gotten off key. We have gone to seed on one particular doctrine to the neglect of the whole gospel. An overemphasis on predestination (a biblical teaching) led some to have an antimissionary spirit. Others have ridden the hobby horse of Neo-pentecostalism, preaching about speaking in tongues and faith healing as if they were the greatest gifts of all. First Corinthians 13 teaches that "love is the greatest of them all" (NEB).

Some people have taught baptismal regeneration when the Bible teaches that we are saved by faith. When we major on the minors, when the church is caught up in controversy, we neglect evangelism and missions. Our faith loses focus, and our vision of Christ and His will become blurry.

It is easy to grow sentimental about Christmas. We can get caught up in Christmas traditions which are at heart harmless but are still basically secular or pagan. It is possible to talk about everybody loving a baby (incidentally, not everyone does). The focus and message of Christmas is the *incarnation*. Our Creator God has entered His world and human history in the person of Jesus. The babe born at Bethlehem was none other than the very Son of God, the eternal God-man. The gospel message itself is here at Christmas. This is the beginning of the gospel: the birth, teachings, death and resurrection of Jesus, and the granting of the Holy Spirit. Nothing, no event is any more at the heart of our faith than the Christmas event.

Our Faith Comes Into Focus . . .

. . . in our worship on Christmas Eve at the Lord's Table. The whole Christ-event had its beginning at Bethlehem, though its origin was in the heart of God. If we could observe the Lord's Supper only once a year, I'd want to do it on Maundy Thursday before Easter Sunday. If we could observe it only twice, I'd choose Christmas Eve for the second.

The Lord's Supper *reveals* the high price of sin—a price too high for us to pay. It reminds us that by His atoning death Jesus paid our sin debt. The price we must pay in our response is commitment to the Christ who loved us so.

The Lord's Supper *recalls* events in the life of Christ: His birth to the virgin Mary at Bethlehem, His unforgettable teachings in the Sermon on the Mount, and His cross set against a darkening sky. Finally, there was an empty tomb and a risen Lord appearing to more than 500 persons. The earthly life of Jesus began in the cave where He was born and ended in the cave in which He was entombed. But that was not the end of the salvation story!

The Lord's Supper calls us to realize the presence of our living Lord. Recall how the two disciples at Emmaus recognized the Lord as He broke the bread at their table and blessed it. This same risen Christ is alive today, and His focused Presence may well be encountered at the table.

On this Christmas Eve let us focus our faith on the Lord Jesus Christ. Let these aids to our worship remind us that He is here in our midst as surely as we are gathered in His name.

- The bread recalls His body sacrificed on the cross.
- The fruit of the vine reminds us of His life's blood shed for our redemption.
- The flame of the Advent candles are symbols of His burning Presence with us—the *shekinah* glory of God.

"Do this in remembrance of me" (Luke 22:19).

SOLO	"Thou Didst Leave Thy Thone"	Matthews
ORDINANCE OF THE LORD'S SUPPER		
Giving of the Bread		
Instrumental Meditation		Cellist
Giving of the Cup		
Anthem	"Child in the Manger"	Bock
LIGHTING OF THE CANDLES		
BENEDICTION		

27
In Our Worth

PRELUDE	"God So Loved the World"	Stainer
HYMN	"Whosoever Will"	Bliss
WELCOME AND PRAYER		
HYMN	"Christ Receiveth Sinful Men"	McGranahan
HYMN	"I've Found a Friend, O Such a Friend"	Stebbins

SERMON   "The Lord's Presence—In Our Worth"
1 John 4:7-11

Visiting at Ohio State University, I saw a memorable painting. It was dark on the left side and grew lighter as you looked to the right. The canvas was covered with many symbols representing the progress of civilization. There were cavemen drawings and Egyptian hiero-glyphics, the owl of Athena and thunderbolt of Zeus, the fluer-de-lis of the Medicis of Italy and kings of France; there was a star of David, a Christian cross, and the crescent of Islam; there was a swastika, dollar mark, and the peace symbol. Famous trademarks were also depicted.

I found the painting impressive and thought-provoking. What are the symbols of Christianity? They are a mustard seed for faith, a cross for salvation, a loaf and cup for communion, and a towel for service.

The cross of Christ speaks eloquently of God's love—and also of our worth. "Love springs from God. . . . He sent his one and only Son." God made us. He is the Creator of our humanity.

It is true that we have the treasure of the gospel in the earthen vessels of our humanity, but we should not despise our human nature. Our bodies are the temple of God's Holy Spirit.

God not only made us; He also sent His only Son to give us salvation and its attendant forgiveness. God loves us, and His love knows no limit. His grace is ours, and we are doubly His. God's love proves our worth.

Others have worth as well. "If God loved *us* that much, then *we* ought to love one another." William Temple contended that "war breaks out when worship breaks down." When we fail to acknowledge the "worthship" of God, we forget to value others as persons. We label them and treat them as objects to be despised or even destroyed. The closer we come to God, the closer we should come to one another.

As we come to observe the Lord's Supper, let us worship God and value other persons, for they are made in His image. Christ died for us all.

When you pass the tray of bread to the worshiper next to you, whisper, "Jesus said, 'This is my body.' " As you pass the tray of cups, whisper, "Jesus said, 'This is my blood.' " Christ gave His all for us.

"Let us love one another."

OBSERVANCE OF THE LORD'S SUPPER
  Giving of the Bread
    Solo   "O Love That Wilt Not Let Me Go"   Caldwell

Giving of the Cup
    Anthem   "I Saw the Cross of Jesus"   Anon.
                         Choir   (Arr. Mayfield)
HYMN   "We Have a Gospel to Proclaim"   Gardiner

28
And Our Salvation

SACRED ORGAN MUSIC "O Sorrow Deep"   Brahms
CALL TO WORSHIP
HYMN   "Love Divine, All Loves Excelling"   Zundel
WORDS OF WELCOME
HYMN   "When I Survey the Wondrous Cross"   Mason
CALL TO PRAYER   Pastoral Prayer
THE MORNING OFFERING
    Anthem   "Rise Up and Sing"   Wagner
              Choir with Descant
    Doxology
    Prayer of Dedication

SERMON
    "The Lord's Presence—And Our Salvation"
    Hebrews 2:1-9a

"How shall we escape if we neglect so great a salvation?" (v. 3).

An unknown Welsh preacher remarked that this text asks a question which no one can answer. The wisest person on earth and the angels in heaven cannot answer this—for there is no escape if we neglect salvation. The word translated "neglect" is a nautical term.

It means to drift like an anchorless ship—toward shipwreck. What an arresting text!

Salvation is both an everyday term and a theological one. Salvation (*soteria*) means deliverance—from danger, illness, or an enemy. In the Old Testament, it was applied to crossing the Red Sea safely. In the New Testament, salvation points to the cross of Christ where our spiritual deliverance was secured. We are saved from sin's tyranny, eternal death, and hell—the greatest dangers.

The Philippian jailor asked, "What must I do to be saved?" Paul's clear answer was, "Believe in the Lord Jesus, and you will be saved" (Acts 16:31).

Dr. Dale Moody contends that salvation has one way, two sides, and three stages.

The One Way of Salvation

The apostles taught that there is "no other name . . . by which we must be saved" (Acts 4:12). The historic Jesus was and is God incarnate (in flesh). He was and is the supreme revelation of God. Christ was and is the cosmic Christ who was before Abraham—He is the Eternal. God "has not left himself without a witness" through the ages (see Acts 14:17). Jesus Christ is the Way to the Father.

The Two Sides of Salvation

John Calvin emphasized the grace of God. Our sin deserved to be punished. God sent His son to atone for sin. God takes the initiative in our salvation. The new birth or regeneration is the work of the Holy Spirit in our lives. From God's side or point of view, salvation is "grace upon grace."

Martin Luther emphasized humanity's faith response to divine love and provision for our salvation. We confess our faith by baptism. God provides, and we believe. Salvation is of grace and by faith. It consists of God's initiative and our response.

The Three Stages of Salvation

Our salvation is a *past* experience. "By grace you have been saved" (Eph. 2:8). "Your faith has saved you" (Luke 7:50). These references are in the past tense. Regeneration represents the beginning of our salvation. At our new birth, we were set free from the penalty of our sin. A Bible translator told about seeking a word or term for redemption in a West African language. He hit upon a phrase which meant "he took our heads out." During the days of human slavery, one could recognize a friend or relative, pay the slave price, and the owner would "take his head out" of the iron collar. The slave was set free. That is sort of what Christ did for us when we were saved. "You are not your own; you were bought with a price" (1 Cor. 6:19-20).

Salvation also has a *present* tense. We are told to "work out your own salvation with fear and trembling; for God is at work in you" (Phil. 2:12-13). We are being saved day-by-day from the power and practice of sin. This is the doctrine of sanctification. We are to grow toward spiritual maturity.

We may also speak of our salvation as a *future* hope. It begins in time but will be brought to completion in eternity. This is the doctrine of glorification. "Our salvation is nearer to us now than when we first believed" (Rom. 13:11). At the last day we will be saved from the presence of sin and evil, temptation and death. "Salvation to be revealed in the last time" (1 Pet. 1:5). Our salvation will be complete when Christ returns in glory.

Christ is present in our salvation. This is a call to persevere in the faith. D. M. Baillie said that we stand between a memory and a hope—looking back to the incarnation and looking forward to the consummation. Come. The Lord's Table is an exciting place to stand.

OBSERVANCE OF THE LORD'S SUPPER
  Giving of the Bread
    Anthem   "As I Grow"   Miller
                          Solist and Choir
  Giving of the Cup "He Came As A Teacher"   Miller
                          Soloist and Choir

HYMN	"Just As I Am, Thine Own to Be"	Barnby
SHARING OF DECISION		Benediction
MOMENT OF SILENCE		Organ Dismissal

29
In the Church

PRELUDE	"The Church's One Foundation"	Wesley
HYMN	"I Am Thine, O Lord"	Doane
WELCOME AND PRAYER		
HYMN	"Tis So Sweet to Trust in Jesus"	Kirkpatrick
ANTHEM	"I Have Come from the Darkness	Arr: Lyall
	Choir	
HYMN	"Heavenly Sunlight"	Cook
SOLO	"Upon This Rock"	Gaither and McGuire

SERMON   "The Lord's Presence—In the Church"

Ephesians 2:19-22; 4:4-6; 1 Peter 2:4-5,9

The church has many critics, within and without. A decade ago, it was in vogue to despise the institutional church. While many have been quick to point out what is wrong with the church, let me invite you to consider what's right with it.

The church is right in its *origin*. It had a right beginning. The church was divinely established, or it would have perished from the face of the earth long ago. It would have gone the way of the Roman mystery religions had it not been based on divine revelation. It is founded on the rock of faith.

The church is right in that is it *ongoing*. The church has survived both persecution and establishment. It is ten times as old as the United

States and exists on every continent, under every type of government and economic system. The church has outlived its enemies from Nero to Nietzsche.

The church is right in that it is more than an organization—it is an *organism*. It has grown across the years from eleven disciples to one billion adherents. It is dynamic and not static. It changes with the times while remaining true to the timeless gospel. The church is the only institution in society which brings persons to encounter the living Christ and then to mature in the faith.

The New Testament word for the church is *ekklesía* from which we obtain the English word *ecclesiastical*. It has two roots. The Hebrew root is is translated "congregation" and describes the people of God *called together* to hear His Word. The Greek root means an "assembly" like the town meeting of a Greek city-state. It describes the *called-out* people of God. Many rich metaphors are used in the New Testament to describe this unique *ekklesía*.

The church is the *body of Christ* which describes our unity, our oneness in Christ. Paul described the church as being one body, one Spirit, one hope; having one Lord, one faith, and one baptism, existing beneath the lordship of God who is the Father of us all, above all, through all, and in all (Eph. 4:5). What a ringing doxology! He piles words on top of one another to describe our sublime unity and oneness.

In my denomination today is Baptist World Alliance Sunday. We recall our unity with 30,000,000 fellow baptized believers in 130 countries of the world. They come from varied backgrounds and live in multiple cultures. Yet we are one in Christ and our loyalty to world missions. The largest group of Baptist believers outside the United States is in the Soviet Union. Add to this host the hundreds of millions of believers in other fellowships. They, too, are our brethren in Christ. The church is in reality one body, the body of Christ.

The church is the *Bride of Christ*. This speaks of His love. Christ loved the church and gave Himself up for her (Eph. 5:25). It is the object of His affection. How dare we despise what Christ so loved?

Our church is a caring fellowship. We love God, and we love one another. The Sunday School classes are where lots of the caring occurs. We also care about those who are outside our fellowship and long to share Christ with them. The church is the company of the caring. Our motto is: "A Caring Church—Proclaiming the Gospel."

The church was also called the *building of God* in Ephesians. This is remarkable when you recall that there were no church buildings in the first century. Thus, Paul is calling the people who make up the church the "building" in which God lives. We constitute "living stones" built on a solid foundation. That substructure is made up of the prophets (special preachers of the Old Testament); the apostles (eyewitnesses to the Christ-event in the New Testament); and our spiritual ancestors in every generation. Christ Himself is the cornerstone in this spiritual structure.

One intriguing fact about the building of God is: it is incomplete, in process. Others are constantly being added to the house of faith. The church is like the Washington Cathedral—longtime a building. The Cathedral was begun in 1907 and will not be finished until 1991. The building of God is also a glorious building, a dwellingplace for God through the Spirit.

Finally, the church constitutes a *royal priesthood* (1 Pet. 2:4-5,9). Our primary purpose is to worship, "offer spiritual sacrifices acceptable to God" (v. 5). We offer Him our bodies as living sacrifices, our ethical life-style, our prayer life and worship. The church's first task is to glorify God.

In addition to leading people in worship, a priest also shares his faith. We are to "declare the wonderful deeds of him who called you out of darkness into marvelous light" (v. 9). We proclaim the mighty acts of God and tell the good news of Christ Jesus.

Once a new convert came to Spurgeon asking what he could do for Christ. The preacher asked the convert's occupation. He was a railroad engineer. Spurgeon asked, "Is your fireman a Christian?" The engineer replied that he didn't know. "Then find out and share your faith with him," replied the preacher.

The church is made up of born-again, baptized believers. It is to be a regenerate group. Are you part of this glorious company?

We cannot destroy the church, but we can fail it. And the church's

future depends on its Founder. "I Love Thy Church, O Lord!" He is
present in His church.

OBSERVANCE OF THE LORD'S SUPPER
  Giving of the Bread
  Giving of the Cup
HYMN   "Living for Jesus"   Lowden

30
In Our Service

SACRED ORGAN MUSIC   "Prelude in A Minor"   Bach
CALL TO WORSHIP
HYMN OF THE CHRISTIAN LIFE
"Serve the Lord with Gladness"   McKinney
WORDS OF WELCOME
SOLO   "O Master, Let Me Walk with Thee"   Smith
SERMON HYMN
"Come, All Christians, Be Committed"   fr. *The Sacred Harp*
SCRIPTURE READING   John 13:14-15
CALL TO PRAYER   Pastoral Prayer
THE MORNING OFFERING
  Anthem "Lord, Make Me an Instrument of Thy Peace"   Rutter
  Congregational Response
      "O Church of God, Triumphant"   Words: Harlow
      (Hymn: "The Church's One Foundation"; Tune: AURELIA)
  Prayer of Dedication

SERMON   "The Lord's Presence—In Our Service"

"Now before the feast of the Passover, when Jesus knew that his hour had come to depart out of this world to the Father, having loved his own who were in the world, he loved them to the end. And during supper, when the devil had already put it into the heart of Judas Iscariot, Simon's son, to betray him, Jesus, knowing that the Father had given all things into his hands, and that he had come from God and was going to God, rose from supper, laid aside his garments, and girded himself with a towel. Then he poured water into a basin, and began to wash the disciples' feet, and to wipe them with the towel with which he was girded. . . .

"When he had washed their feet, and taken his garments, and resumed his place, he said to them, 'Do you know what I have done to you? You call me Teacher and Lord; and you are right, for so I am. If I then, your Lord and Teacher, have washed your feet, you also ought to wash one another's feet. For I have given you an example, that you also should do as I have done to you' " (John 13:1-5,12-15).

There are many symbols of our faith. One of these is the towel of service.

The Wrong Kind of Service

It is possible to do the right thing for the wrong reason. Our service even in the church may have selfish motivation. We may take a job or even perform a ministry for the gratification of our ego. We may do it for show, recognition, or applause. Most all of us have the show-off instinct. We may serve others for power, praise, or "perks."

Somehow we have managed to make the biblical word *charity* into a bad word. We may help others in a condescending or patronizing fashion. By this we clearly see ourselves as their superiors, and we look down on them. Such an attitude was never characteristic of Jesus. Though He was rich He became poor for our sake. He emptied Himself of His divine prerogatives and became obedient—even to death.

We are more like the disciples than the Master. We, too, want to be the greatest in the kingdom. Jesus taught that true greatness is one of function, not of status; of service, not a position of power.

Jesus gave us an example of . . .

The Right Kind of Service

Recall the scene in the upper room. It was Thursday of Jesus' last week just prior to His arrest, trials, and crucifixion. The Gospel writer tells us what Jesus was thinking that night.

- Jesus was aware that His hour had come. Repeatedly during His ministry He had said in effect, "Not yet." Now the time for His atoning death was at hand.

- Jesus was also conscious of His mission. He knew He had come from God and was going to God. His Messianic consciousness was high.

- Jesus cared about His disciples. He loved His own. They were an odd lot. Jesus had imperfect tools with which to work. The kingdom treasure was in "earthen vessels," and it still is.

The Master taught His disciples a lesson in humility by an acted parable. He arose from the table, wrapped a long towel around His waist, and filled a basin with water. Jesus proceeded to wash the grimy feet of His disciple circle. He, their Teacher, performed a slave's task for them. It must have been a shocking and memorable experience. Surely they must have remembered Jesus' dramatic action as long as they lived.

In the kingdom of God, service is the measure of greatness! Jesus becomes real and present with us when we serve in His name and spirit.

How Do We Apply the Principle of Service?

Richard Foster wrote about "the grace of humility." Like happiness, humility is a serendipity, a by-product of usefulness. We serve not to show but for Christ and others. It is as simple as giving a cup of cold water in Christ's name. A leper in Korea sang the song, "Where he leads me I will follow." Because part of his lip was gone, the leper pronounced "leads" as "needs." Christian service means going where we are needed.

There is to be a hiddenness to our service. It includes anonymity. Much can be accomplished when we are no longer concerned about who gets the credit for what is done.

The "eleventh commandment" is that we "love one another" (John 13:34). That love ideally is unselfish, sacrificial, and forgiving. "They will know we are Christians by our love."

Don't wait to be asked—drafted. Volunteer for Christian service. Let us be inducted into the "Order of the Towel." Jesus taught His disciples that night, "I have given you an example that you should do as I have done."

The Lord's Supper is a symbol of service. Christ comes to us as we serve.

OBSERVANCE OF THE LORD'S SUPPER
  Giving of the Bread
  Giving of the Cup
HYMN OF INVITATION   "O Master, Let Me Walk with Thee"
                                                            Smith
SHARING OF DECISIONS   Benediction
MOMENT OF SILENCE   Organ Dismissal

31
In Our Memories

PRELUDE   "O Sorrow Deep"   Brahms
                       "Libera Me"   Faure
CALL TO WORSHIP   "O Come and Mourn with Me"   Burroughs
                    Sanctuary Ensemble

OPENING PRAYER
HYMN MEDLEY   Congregation
        Rock of Ages, cleft for me,
        Let me hide myself in thee;
        Let the water and the blood
        From Thy wounded side which flowed,

Be of sin the double cure,
Save from wrath and make me pure.   Hastings

Jesus, keep me near the cross,
There a precious fountain,
Free to all, a healing stream,
Flows from Calv'ry's mountain.
In the cross, in the cross/ Be my glory ever,
Till my ransomed soul shall find
Rest beyond the river.
Near the cross! O Lamb of God,
Bring its scenes before me;
Help me walk from day to day.
With its shadow o'er me.
In the cross, in the cross/ Be my glory ever,
Till my ransomed soul shall find
Rest beyond the river.   Doane

A Service of Shadows

1. Shadow of Betrayal
   Matthew 26:20-25
   Solo   "Hymn of the Last Supper"   Demarest
2. Shadow of Desertion
   Matthew 26:30-35
                 "There Is a Green Hill Far Away"   Stebbins
   Solo: Stanzas 1 and 2
   Congregation: Stanza 3
                 There was no other good enough
                   To pay the price of sin,
                 He only could unlock the gate
                   Of heaven and let us in.
                 Oh, dearly, dearly has He loved,
                   And we must love Him, too,
                 And trust in His redeeming blood,
                   and try His works to do.

3. Shadow of an Unshared Vigil
    Luke 22:39-46
    Organ Meditation   "I Stand Amazed in the Presence"

                                                    Words: Lutkin

    (Hymn: "Into the Woods My Master Went," Tune: LANIER)

            For me it was in the garden He prayed,
                "Not my will, but Thine."
            He had no tears for His own griefs,
            But sweat drops of blood for mine.

4. Shadow of Accusation
    Mark 14:57-65
    Reading

            My song is love unknown,/ My Savior's love to me,
            Love to the loveless shown,
            That they might lovely be.
            O who am I,
            That for my sake
            My Lord should take,/ Frail flesh and die?
            He came from his blest throne,
            Salvation to bestow:
            But men made strange, and none
            The longed-for Christ would know.
            But O my Friend,/ My Friend indeed,
            Who at my need/ His life did spend!
            Sometimes they strew his way,
            And his sweet praises sing;
            Resounding all the day/ Hosannas to their King.
            Then "Crucify!"/ Is all their breath,
            And for his death/ They thirst and cry.[20]

5. Shadow of Crucifixion
    Matthew 27:27-38
    Hymn   "Man of Sorrows"   Bliss
    Luke 23:44-47   Minister
                            Stanzas 3,4   Congregation

6. MEDITATION

"The Lord's Presence—In Our Memory"

"Do this in remembrance of me" (1 Cor. 11:24).

Memory is an important asset. It is our collective consciousness—how we know who we are. The poet wrote that God gave us memory, so we could have roses in December. That is a nice sentiment, but a greenhouse will do that.

Memory gives us a sense of history, our origin, roots, and identity. By it we relive special events: birthdays, anniversaries, and days of national significance. The Lord's Supper is a call to remember Christ and the cross.

Memory relives past events, focusing on their significance. Note the strong verbs in the account of the Supper's institution. Jesus "took bread, . . . blessed, . . . broke it, . . . gave it to the disciples" (Matt. 26:26).

Recall the events of Jesus' suffering (called the Passion): Hear the cries of the crowd and Pilate's protest of innocence; see Judas' dark kiss of betrayal; listen to the crack of a whip, the thud of a hammer, and a cry of anguish from the cross; recall the towering crosses silhouetted against that angry Judean sky; hear the sobs of His brokenhearted mother and later those of Simon Peter.

"It was for me he died, on Calvary." Thanks be to God!

Memory teaches who Jesus is: both son of Mary and Son of God. It recalls why He came: to show us the Father's limitless love, "to seek and to save the lost" (Luke 19:10). Like the penitent thief we want to pray, "Lord, remember me" (Luke 23:42, KJV).

Memory also teaches us where Jesus is. He is interceding on our behalf at the Father's right hand—remembering us. He is indwelling believers with the Holy Spirit. Jesus is our inspiration here at the Lord's table. He is present with us in our remembrance and observance. His spiritual power is ours. Joy!

Come, let us remember the Lord Christ, as He commanded.

7. OBSERVANCE OF THE LORD'S SUPPER
   The Bread
   Anthem   "Surely He Hath Borne Our Griefs"   Graun
                         Ensemble
   The Cup
   Anthem   "Blessed Lord, All Love Excelling"   Liszt
CLOSING PRAYER
CHORAL RESPONSE   "Thee We Adore, O Savior"   Dubois

32
In Time

PRELUDE   "Forward Through the Ages"   Sullivan
HYMN   "Blessed Be the Name"   Hudson
PRAYER AND WELCOME
ANTHEM   "O Day of Rest and Gladness"   Arr. Burroughs
                         Choir
THE EVENING OFFERING
   Offertory Anthem "If Ye Love Me, Keep My Commandments"
                                                        Tallis

   Offertory Prayer
HYMN   "Amazing Grace, How Sweet the Sound"   fr.: Va.
                                                       Harmony

SERMON   "The Lord's Presence—In Time"

1 Corinthians 10:1-4,16-17

"So, whether you eat or drink, or whatever you do, do all to the glory of God" (1 Cor. 10:31).

During the Middle Ages, great Gothic cathedrals were built in

Europe. Many lovely stories come from this time of faith. One of these is a legend that God would reward the person who worked best in the construction of one of those mammoth church buildings. There was considerable speculation about who would be chosen. Would it be the architect, the master builder, or the craftsmen in stone, glass, gold, or bronze? Each did his best and awaited the announcement of the heavenly commendation. All were surprised when the best worker turned out to be an old peasant woman who had carried fodder each day for the ox that pulled the sled for the masons.

This old story reminds us that everybody is somebody in the sight of the Lord. He looks not on outward appearances but on the inner motivation of our hearts. Everyone counts, matters, and is loved by God. We also want to remember that every person can serve the Lord, no matter how high or humble his or her position in life. Therefore, we are to use our time wisely and live for His glory in our business or professional lives, in the factory or classroom, and in our homes and churches.

All Life Is Sacred

God made the world, and He made us. He is the Lord of life. Therefore, the Scriptures say: "In all thy ways acknowledge him, and he shall direct thy paths" (Prov. 3:6, KJV). "In everything by prayer and supplication with thanksgiving let your requests be made known to God" (Phil. 4:6), and "Whatever you do, do all to the glory of God" (1 Cor. 10:31).

God comes to us amid the ordinary. It is sometimes hard to be aware of His Presence when life is so routine. We take the children to school, choir rehearsal, or a dental appointment. There is housework to be done, luncheons to attend, letters and notes to write, phone calls to be made, lessons worked on, lawns mowed, and the inevitable "honey-do-this" list. Who can be aware of God's presence in the midst of such mundane activities? Remember that He was born in a Bethlehem stable, grew up in a small town, and spent thirty years working in a carpenter's shop. We know He was well acquainted with the ordinary. Note where He went for His illustrations and parables: sowing, fishing, making bread; birds, spring wild flowers, and sheep.

Jesus fulfilled His Father's will and was aware of the divine presence in the midst of the ordinary. So may we.

God also reveals Himself and His purpose in the extraordinary, special times. These are events filled with a meaning for us, whether happy times or sad. They may be events like marriage, the birth of a child, a promotion or honor, a new home or car, retirement or bereavement, or in a time of accident or illness when we are put flat on our backs and have no way to look except up. God is near us in the crisis times as well as the routine. The Holy Spirit can make us sensitive to His leading and His help, even then.

Worship Is an Especially Sacred Time

An estimated 50,000,000 Americans attend church on any given Sunday. While their motives are many, surely the worship of God is the dominant one. No worship experience has a greater potential to be more sacred or blessed than the observance of the Lord's Supper.

The Supper reminds us that God is near and accessible. We can approach Him boldly. Suppose you could pray only once a year or observe the ordinance only once a year (as some Scottish churches do)? Wouldn't you want to make sincere spiritual preparation for such an occasion? Then why do we pray and come to the Lord's table so casually? At Saint Peter's Basilica in Rome there is a "Porta Sancta" or holy door which is opened only one year in twenty-five. Only twice in a lifetime will a pilgrim be apt to enter the largest church in the world through that door. Suppose we were able to enter into the presence of the Lord only twice in a lifetime. These illustrations make us think about the blessed privilege which is ours in worship and prayer.

At the Lord's Table He comes to us in the symbols of the ordinary bread and cup. These simple elements stand for the extraordinary— the body and blood of Jesus Christ. God is near to us and accessible in the observance. Often we fret like the women on Easter morning en route to the garden tomb. They were worried about who would roll the stone away from the tomb for them. God had already rolled it away, opening up the secret of the resurrection. Remember how the angel sent word to Jesus' disciples by the women that he was going before "them into Galilee" (Matt. 28:7). Our God is always out before us, preparing the way, leading us.

There are certain prayers which God always answers in the affirmative. One is this: "Lord Jesus, come into my heart, right now, and forever. Have your way in my life." Another is: "Not my will, but thine, be done" (Luke 22:42).

Come, let us worship God around His table.

THE LORD'S SUPPER
   Giving of the Bread
   Giving of the Cup
HYMN   "Blest Be the Tie"   Mason
BENEDICTION   Organ Dismissal

33
In His Gifts

SACRED ORGAN MUSIC   "Prelude in Variations"   de Cabezon
CALL TO WORSHIP
HYMN   "All Hail the Power of Jesus' Name"   Shrubsole
CALL TO PRAYER   Pastoral Prayer
HYMN   "Amazing Grace, How Sweet the Sound"   from Va.
                                                          Harmony
WORDS OF WELCOME
THE MORNING OFFERING
   Anthem   "The Lord is My Shepherd"   Matthews
                              Choir
   Congregational Response
        "How Sweet the Name of Jesus Is"   words: Newton

(Hymn: "Majestic Sweetness Sits Enthroned," tune: ORTON-
VILLE)
Jesus, my shepherd, brother, friend,/ My prophet, priest and
king,
   My Lord, my life, my way, my end,
   Accept the praise I bring,/ Accept the praise I bring.
Responsive Prayer of Dedication

Leader: Lord, our God, let joy grip all who give and gratitude,
all who receive.

People: May all littleness of spirit, appearance of greed, and
expression of vanity not be found among us.

Leader: May this offering be found in the place of greatest need
for the spread of Thy Will and the appropriation of Thy
Love.

People: Amen.[21]

SERMON   "The Lord's Presence—In His Gifts"
Psalm 23

(Have the congregation recite Psalm 23 from memory.)

This is the psalm of psalms, almost everyone's favorite. We learned
it as children, and it has become a lifelong treasure. It is a moving
affirmation of personal faith and trust in God. Psalm 23 is about our
grateful response to the goodness of God.

I found the Psalms to be like spinach as a youngster. When I was
a boy, I tried to each spinach, but I did not like the taste. I was told
it was good for me, that it would make me strong. For forty years I
did not eat spinach. Then I was served a fresh spinach salad and fell
in love with it. I now grow it each spring.

When I was in my teens, a lady in my home church told me how
much the Psalms meant to her. I read them, but they seemed dull
compared to the travels of Abraham, the story of David and Goliath,
Samuel's call, or Jesus' parables. But as I've grown older, the Psalms
have become a source of spiritual nurture. I've come to love them.

Let us walk through Psalm 23 in an expository fashion. "The Lord is my shepherd" (v. 1). He is not only the Keeper of the nation but *my* personal Shepherd as well. This truth implies that we are sheep—this is not exactly a compliment. They are not the smartest members of the animal kingdom.

To call the Lord our Shepherd means:

He *provides* for us, "green pastures . . . still waters . . . he restores my soul" (refreshes my life).

The Lord *guides* us. "He leads me in paths of righteousness [right paths] for his name's sake" (v. 3). He directs us to make correct decisions, wise choices.

God also *comforts* us, "Even though I walk through the valley of the shadow of death" (v. 4). This is not a reference to death *per se.* The Hebrew is translated "the valley of deep darkness" or "the valley of dark shadows." This can refer to any experience which threatens us or is filled with danger. It can be a health problem, a financial or job loss, or a problem within the family, as well as a life-threatening situation. Whatever frightens or threatens us can be our "valley of the shadow."

Dr. Clarence Cranford of Washington, DC, told about a father who sent his young son to put the milk bottles out on the porch one night for the milkman's pickup. The lad was frightened and protested, "It's too dark to go out there without a father." We feel much the same about our dark experiences.

The psalmist affirmed his faith saying, "I will fear no evil: for thou art with me" (v. 4, KJV). We are never really alone. "Thy rod and thy staff, they comfort me." This was stern stuff—the shepherd's weapons. But they were for the sheep's protection and thus were a comfort. God is our Protector.

In the final two verses (5 and 6) of the psalm, the metaphor shifts to: the Lord is my Host. The scene is a banquet table, a sumptuous supper, a feast. We are safe at the Lord's table even in the presence of our enemies. God provides the very best, and that in abundance. This banquet is not on the rubber-chicken circuit with its unearthly green and inedible beans or peas!

Note the Lord's gracious hospitality: "Thou anointest my head with oil," sweetly perfumed oil, as a sign of His welcome (v. 5). Note also His generous provision: "my cup runneth over" (KJV). *The Jerusalem Bible* translates this verse, "my cup brims over." The Lord's portions are not skimpy but generous, abundant, and extravagant.

Recall that when the prodigal son returned from the far country, they killed the fatted calf and had a joyous banquet. The prodigal's father said, "It was fitting to make merry and be glad" (Luke 15:32).

The psalmist sang, "Surely goodness and mercy shall follow me all the days of my life." God's mercy is *hesed* in the Hebrew. This word describes the Lord's loving-kindness or covenant love. It is the love which grows out of a relationship with the Father. You can count on His love. It is dependable and knows no limits.

The goodness and love of God will literally *pursue* us. God is no reluctant Deity. We do not have to "storm heaven in '87." Our Father is anxious to bless us, ready and willing—more ready than we are—to answer our prayers.

An unknown Scottish preacher spoke of this passage, "The Lord is my Shepherd, aye, and He has two fine collie dogs, 'goodness and mercy.' And they will see me safely home!"

"And I shall dwell in the house of the Lord for ever" (v. 6). This means to be in the divine Presence, with the Lord always. Surely that is the essence of heaven. What a psalm of affirmation and trust!

As we prepare to observe the Lord's Supper, let us remember that it foreshadows the heavenly banquet. Jesus promised to eat it with us one day in the kingdom of God.

Focus on the anointing with oil. This symbolizes our glad reception by the Father. We are restored, and our sins are forgiven. The overflowing cup stands for God's abundant gifts and provision. He has given us all we need and more. God is gracious—forgiving our sins. God is generous—providing our needs. Our response should be a life-style of gratitude. Recall that Jesus said of the woman who anointed His feet, "They who are forgiven love much" (Luke 7:47).

God provides us with all the necessities of life: air, water, food, and moderate temperature. All of these are absent in outer space. Our astronauts have to carry their life-support system into space with them. Yet we tend to take for granted clean air, safe water, and abundant good food.

In addition to all these necessities, the Lord gives us many extras. These include things such as *color:* scarlet and gold cannas, a sunset, dogwood, tulips and azaleas, roses and impatiens. What if the world were dull black and white with no color?

Another extra is *sound:* the song of a mockingbird, the sound of the wind in pine trees, and the pounding of the surf. What if there were a "silent spring" due to a nuclear holocaust?

Fragrance is another extra: the fragrance of food, honeysuckle, and magnolia blossoms.

There are many human extras as well: a baby's smile, a child's curiosity, people whose thoughtfulness makes you feel special. Helen Keller was blind and deaf. She learned to communicate through touch. She wrote that she found shaking hands with people to be an eloquent experience. Some people seemed devoid of joy, and their fingertips were frosty. Keller noted, however, that other people's hands seemed to have a sunbeam in them, and their grasp warmed her heart.

The psalmist knew and celebrated God's extras—His overflowing, abundant blessings. Life's extras are meant to bring us to God. They elicit our gratitude and our trust.

God's "unspeakable gift" (2 Cor. 9:15, KJV) is celebrated now in our observance of the Lord's Supper. His Presence is evident in His many gifts to us.

OBSERVANCE OF THE LORD'S SUPPER
    Giving of the Bread
Instrumental Meditation   "My Shepherd Will Supply My Need"
                                                  Arr. Thompson
    Giving of the Cup
      Solo   "I Saw the Cross of Jesus"   Arr. Manuel
HYMN   "Blest Be the Tie"   Mason
SHARING OF DECISIONS
BENEDICTION   MOMENT OF SILENCE   ORGAN DISMISSAL

34
In Our Eating

PRELUDE
HYMN   "I Am Thine, O Lord"   Doane
WELCOME AND PRAYER
THE EVENING OFFERING
    Solo   "Let Us Break Bread Together"   Traditional Spiritual
    Prayer of Dedication
HYMN   "When We Walk with the Lord"   Towner
RESPONSIVE READING   Revelation 22:7-14 (KJV)

Leader: Behold, I come quickly:

People: blessed is he that keepeth the sayings of the prophecy of the book.

Leader: And I John saw these things and heard them.

People: And when I had heard and seen, I fell down to worship before the feet of the angel which shewed me these things.

Leader: Then saith he unto me, See thou do it not:

People: for I am thy fellowservant, and of thy brethren the prophets, and of them which keep the sayings of this book:

Leader: Worship God.

People: And he saith unto me, Seal not the sayings of the prophecy of this book: for the time is at hand.

Leader: He that is unjust, let him be unjust still: and he which is filthy, let him be filthy still:

People: and he that is righteous, let him be righteous still: and he that is holy, let him be holy still.

Leader: And, behold, I come quickly;

People: and my reward is with me, to give every man according as his work shall be.

Leader: I am Alpha and Omega, the beginning and the end, the first and the last.

All: Blessed are they that do his commandments, that they may have right to the tree of life, and may enter in through the gates into the city.

SERMON "The Lord's Presence—In Our Eating
Exodus 24:9-11

"Moses went up with Aaron, Nadab and Abihu, and seventy elders of Israel. They saw the God of Israel beneath whose feet there was, it seemed, a sapphire pavement pure as the heavens themselves. He laid no hand on these notables of the sons of Israel: they gazed on God. They ate and they drank" (Ex. 24:9-11, *Jerusalem Bible*).

Picture the scene at Mount Sinai. The Hebrews were encamped at the foot of the mountain, freshly freed from enslavement in Egypt. At God's initiative they had received the Commandments and entered into covenant with Him. There were two ceremonies to seal the new covenant relationship.

At the foot of the mountain, the people gathered to hear a word from God. They pledged to obey the Commandments. They erected twelve stones to symbolize the twelve tribes of Israel. An animal was sacrificed as an act of worship, and its blood was sprinkled, half on the altar and half toward the people. The Old Covenant was sealed with the blood of a sacrificed animal. The New Covenant would be sealed with the blood of Christ, shed for the atonement of sins.

The second ceremony symbolizing the covenant took place on the mountain. There Moses, three priests, and the seventy elders "gazed on God." They looked up to the sapphire blue sky where God dwelt. God "did not lay His hand on them"; He did not strike them dead. Then they "ate and they drank" (v. 11) a covenant meal before the Lord. It was no ordinary meal but one *eaten in the presence of God.*

The obvious parallel is the Lord's Supper, the symbolic meal of the New Covenant. The Jewish Passover meal commemorates the Exodus of the Israelites from Egyptian bondage. The Christian observance of the Lord's Supper commemorates the Cross-event and the presence of the risen Christ. Both are symbolic meals—eaten before or in the presence of the Lord.

Eating and Drinking Before the Lord Means Friendship with God

He is approachable. You may recall that the riddle asked by the Sphinx was: "Is the universe friendly?" Jesus taught us to call God "Abba," dear Father (Rom. 8:15). Heaven knows us and our needs and cares about us. "My best friend is Jesus."

We celebrate the great times of our lives "before the Lord." Christian marriage takes place "in the sight of God." We are aware of the Almighty as the Giver of life at the birth of our children. We worship, aware that we are in the divine Presence. Baptism is observed in the name of God the Father, Son, and Holy Spirit. The Lord's Supper is eaten with a keen awareness that we are in the focused Presence. At death, we acknowledge that our loved ones are "absent from the body, present with the Lord."

Remember that our relationship with God through Christ is all of grace. We do not deserve it, and we enter it at God's initiative. We eat and drink before the Lord and remember He is our Friend.

Eating and Drinking Together Symbolizes Fellowship

This is a common meal using ordinary food. The Lord's Supper is also a common meal in that we share it in common with our fellow believers. It symbolizes our one faith and our fellowship of love. Normally, we eat only with people whom we like, not with enemies. Eating together at the Lord's Table is a sign of our fellowship with spiritual kinsfolk. In this sense, the Supper is a two-way communion: vertically with God and horizontally with our fellow Christians. One of the hymns of the church speaks about this, "We mystic sweet communion find with those whose race is run." Thus we have fellow-

ship with those present in the service and with those believers who
have gone on before us into glory.

The eating of this symbolic meal before the Lord calls for our
dedication, first to Christ who said, "Do this in remembrance of me"
(Luke 22:19), then to one another. In some services Christians "pass
the peace." They will say, "Peace be with you." The worshiper replies,
"And also with you."

They saw God on Mount Sinai and ate and drank.

So may we eat and drink in His Presence.

ORDINANCE OF THE LORD'S SUPPER
   Giving of the Bread
      Solo   "There Is a Green Hill Far Away"   Stebbins
   Giving of the Cup
Anthem   "If Ye Love Me, Keep My Commandments"   Tallis
                               Choir
HYMN   "Blest Be The Tie"   Mason

35
In Our Bodies

SACRED ORGAN MUSIC   "Von Himmel Hoch"   Karg Elert
CALL TO WORSHIP
HYMN   "When Morning Gilds the Skies"   Barnby
WORDS OF WELCOME
CALL TO PRAYER   Pastoral Prayer
HYMN   "When I Survey the Wondrous Cross"   Mason
THE MORNING OFFERING AND FELLOWSHIP OFFERING
   Anthem   "O Cast Thy Burden Upon the Lord"   Aulbach
                    Ensemble
   Congregational Response

All things are Thine: no gift have we,/ Lord of all gifts, to offer Thee; And hence with grateful hearts today,/ Thine own before Thy feet we lay. Amen.

Prayer of Dedication

SERMON   "The Lord's Presence—In Our Bodies"
                        1 Corinthians 11:24

The last verses from 1 Corinthians 6 read, "Do you not know that your body is a temple of the Holy Spirit within you, which you have from God. You are not your own; you were bought with a price. So glorify God in your body" (vv. 19-20).

In 1 Corinthians 11:24 Jesus is quoted as saying: "This is my body which is for you."

First Corinthians is the oldest document in our New Testament, and this is the earliest account in the Bible of the institution of the Lord's Supper. Still, it was not original with the Apostle Paul. He wrote, "I received from the Lord what I also delivered" (v. 23). The observance of the Lord's Supper was already a stated fact by the time Paul wrote his first Corinthian letter. Doubtless, one of his sources had been the disciples who had been present that night in the upper room at the last Supper. "This," said Jesus, "is my body," as He held up the bread. John quoted Jesus as saying, "He who eats my flesh and drinks my blood has eternal life, and I will raise him up at the last day" (1 Cor. 6:54). The human body is a focus of the Lord's Supper.

The New Testament word for body is *soma* from which we get the medical term *psychosomatic*—involving both mind and body. The body is essential. The body without the spirit is a corpse. The spirit without the body is a ghost. The body is so essential in Hebrew and biblical thought that we believe in the resurrection of the body.

The ancient Greeks despised their bodies. They called the body "the prison house of the soul," or "the tomb of the soul." Some despise the body, and others glorify the body. During the Renaissance the human form was glorified, both male and female. We see this expressed in the paintings and sculpture of artists like Michelangelo. We still glorify the human body with beauty contests. But let's face it—no one is a *10*. Some of the most beautiful people I know aren't necessarily physically attractive.

What do we make of the body? C. S. Lewis said that he considered the human body to be one of God's jokes. I have heard the giraffe described as one of God's mistakes. Lewis commented that we are composite creatures, both rational and irrational—akin on the one side to the angels and on the other to the tomcats. But the Bible teaches the incarnation of God in Jesus Christ. "The Word became flesh and dwelt among us." "The Word became a human being and," the *Good News Bible* translates it, "lived among us" (John 1:14). Jesus could say of the broken bread, "This is my body." If the human body is a joke, then God played the joke on Himself.

Think of that bread. Every piece that we received will be broken, as was His body. Think about the brokenness of bread. First, farmers break up the ground in order to plant the wheat. Then, they go in and harvest the wheat. It is threshed to beat the kernels out of the husks. Then the wheat is taken to the mill and ground. It is crushed into flour. Finally, it is baked into bread and broken again in order to be consumed. The broken bread is a powerful symbol of the body of Christ in our communion service. As we eat this broken bread, through the process of metabolism, it becomes a part of us. We also appropriate the living Christ.

The New Testament teaches that our bodies can be redeemed, received into Christ. The New Testament teaches that this body can become the very dwelling place of God, the Holy Spirit. It also teaches that Christ is in you and me "the hope of glory" (Col. 1:27). We become "living sacrifices" involved in a life of service, obedient to the heavenly vision. The Bible speaks of the church as the body of Christ. We are many, yet we are one body in Christ, and Christ is head of the body, the church.

First Corinthians 15 is the greatest chapter in the Bible about the resurrection—our resurrection. We are told that while we live in this mortal body, one day it is going to be planted, and it is going to rise an immortal, glorified, transformed, resurrection body—from a joke to glory; from imperfection to perfection; from age to eternal life; from deterioration to completion.

Let us eat and drink with gratitude in remembrance of Him who said, "He who eats my flesh . . . has eternal life, and I will raise him up at the last day" (John 6:54).

OBSERVANCE OF THE LORD'S SUPPER
  Giving of the Bread
    Solo   "The Nail-Scarred Hand"   arr. Bass
  Giving of the Cup
    Anthem   "None Other Lamb"   Marshall
                              Choir and Cello
HYMN   "Beneath the Cross of Jesus"   Maker
SHARING OF DECISIONS   Benediction
MOMENT OF SILENCE   Organ Dismissal

36
At Mount Sinai

SACRED ORGAN MUSIC   "What God Ordains Is Always Good"
                                                              Walther
CALL TO WORSHIP   "O Thou Whose Hand Hath Brought Us"
                                                                Webb
                            Choir
O Thou whose hand hath brought us/ Unto this joyful day, Accept our glad thanksgiving,/ And listen as we pray;/ And may our preparation/ For this day's service be/ With one accord to offer ourselves, O Lord, to Thee. . . ./ And oft as here we gather,/ And hearts in worship blend,/ May truth reveal its power,/ And fervent prayer ascend;/ Here may the busy toiler/ Rise to the things above;/ The Young, the old be strengthened,/ And all men learn Thy love. Amen.
OPENING SENTENCES

HYMN OF ADORATION
                "Come, Thou Fount of Every Blessing"   Wyeth
WORDS OF WELCOME
CONCERNS OF THE CONGREGATION
HYMN OF CONSECRATION
                    "I Am Thine, O Lord"   Doane
CALL TO PRAYER
PASTORAL PRAYER
THE MORNING OFFERING
   Duet   "The King of Love My Shepherd Is"   Shelley
   Gloria Patri
   Prayer of Dedication
READING OF THE SCRIPTURE   Exodus 19:1-8

SERMON   "The Lord's Presence—At Mount Sinai"

The Sinai is a beautiful, if inhospitable, piece of real estate. The
brilliant sun glistens on red granite mountains, and multicolored sand
flows in waves fashioned by the wind. There is scant vegetation and
a quietness like that on the surface of the moon. The Israelis and
Egyptians have fought over the Sinai in recent years.

All was not quiet at Sinai after the Exodus. The Hebrew slaves, only
ninety days out of Egypt, were encamped at the foot of Mount Horeb,
the mountain of God, which was also called Mount Sinai. It towered
7500 feet, looming above the surrounding plain. The Hebrews spent
eleven months camped there while Moses negotiated with God on the
mountain.

Moses was a prophet, priest, and national leader. He was a unique
personality in human history. He met God again on the very mountain where he had experienced His call. There he received the Law and
cut a covenant between the Lord God Jehovah and Israel. Sinai was
more than a place, a geographical location. It was an event, an encounter, a happening. It witnessed the birth of a nation and the giving
of God's law for humanity.

Sinai Was an Invitation to Meet God

Note the initiating word: "The Lord called" (v. 3). He appeared to Moses on the mountain—a theophany. He said, "You have seen what I did in Egypt" (v. 4). God delivered them from Pharaoh and bondage, and He delivered them from destruction at the sea. God spoke through Moses, "Therefore, . . . obey my voice and keep my covenant" (v. 5).

The "cutting" of a covenant was an important act. The word for covenant *berith* occurs 286 times in the Old Testament. It literally means "to bind." We still speak of a binding contract. It could be an agreement between two men such as David and Jonathan. The word was also used of a treaty between two nations. A covenant was "cut" by sacrificing an animal. The sacrifice was then cut into pieces. The pieces were placed in two parallel rows, and the parties walked between them. Originally, this probably symbolized the seriousness of the covenant: "If I fail to keep my part of the bargain, may I be cut into pieces." The meat was then cooked and eaten by both parties. Modern contracts are ratified in a simpler fashion: we sign an agreement and shake hands. The covenant on Sinai was sealed with a meal as the elders "ate before the Lord." (Ex. 24:1-11). In much the same way, the New Covenant is symbolized as we eat and drink at the Lord's Supper.

God chose Israel with His electing love. This love was called *chesed* or steadfast, covenant love. He agreed to be their God and promised that they would be a "holy nation," uniquely dedicated to God; Israel would also be a "kingdom of priests" (Ex. 19:6). This meant they would have ready access to God, and they would represent God to the nations. Peter wrote about this same theme by declaring that believers constitute "a royal priesthood, a holy nation" (1 Pet. 2:5-9). The condition in Israel's covenant with God was that they promised to obey His laws.

The covenant was all of grace. God took the initiative to establish it. It was a covenant between unequals, not equals (like that between a king and his vassals). Israel had done nothing to merit God's covenant love. They were, in actuality, no great nation or righteous people.

They had no claim on divine love. It was totally undeserved. So is His love for us. We are sinners and yet the object of His grace. Therefore, we submit gladly to His will and live in gratitude for His love. Think of it! God loved you from before the beginning of history. He sent His Son in the midst of history to die for you. And His love came into your heart at the moment you believed. It is all of grace. If we got what we deserved, we certainly wouldn't be here now.

Sinai Was Also an Invitation to an Ethical Life-Style

The covenant calls for right conduct. "Now, therefore." Someone said to a group of religious enthusiasts: "It isn't how high you jump when you are saved that counts. It's how straight you walk when you hit the ground!"

At Mount Sinai God gave His Law. The Hebrew word for law is "torah." It means "instruction" or "that which points the way." We call this law the Ten Commandments (not the Ten Suggestions). They are stated in short declaratory sentences. They are straight to the point and easily memorized. The Commandments are the basis of all law in the Western world. They are written into the codes of many states and nations.

The first three Commandments relate to God: God comes first, you shall worship no graven images, and do not take God's name in vain (that is more than a prohibition of cursing. It means you shall not bear the name of God for nothing).

The third and fourth Commandments relate to time: remember that the Sabbath is sacred, keep it holy; and remember to honor your parents, the older generation.

The last five Commandments concern man's relations with others: life is sacred—do no murder; sex is sacred—commit no adultery; property is sacred—do not steal; truth is sacred—tell no lies. The last Commandment is perhaps the hardest to keep: do not covet anything.

These Commandments are a discipline. Restraint was necessary—for those former slaves, and for modern nations. Life without restraints is miserable. A national newsmagazine described life inside a sex parlor in New York City. Sex there was jaded and cheap. There was a total lack of relationship to give it meaning. Partners were prohibited from exchanging phone numbers. It was altogether casual, and pathetic.

Faith has a minus as well as a plus. Paul wrote that we are to "put off" our old sins and "put on" Christ.

Elton Trueblood summarized the Ten Commandments in poetic fashion:

Above all else love God alone;/ Bow down to neither wood nor stone./ God's name refuse to take in vain;/ The Sabbath rest with care maintain./ Respect your parents all your days;/ Hold sacred human life always./ Be loyal to your chosen mate;/ Steal nothing, neither small or great./ Report, with truth, your neighbor's deed;/ And rid your mind of selfish greed.[22]

The Hebrews responded, "All that the Lord has spoken we will do (Ex. 19:8).

The prophet Jeremiah promised that one day the Lord would establish a "new covenant," not on stone but within the human heart (Jer. 31:31).

Jesus, at the institution of the Lord's Supper, took the cup and said, "This cup which is poured out for you is the new covenant in my blood" (Luke 22:20).

God invites you to a covenant relationship with Himself. If you will believe with your heart and confess with your mouth that Jesus is the Christ, you will be saved.

The New Covenant is entered through faith in Christ. It constitutes a call to believe and an ethical life-style—*both!*

ORDINANCE OF THE LORD'S SUPPER

Giving of the Bread
    Anthem   "O Sacred Head, Now Wounded"   Bach
Giving of the Cup
    Duet   "Jesus, Savior"   Mozart

HYMN OF INVITATION
            "O Jesus, I Have Promised"   Mann

FELLOWSHIP OFFERING
SHARING OF DECISIONS   Benediction
MOMENT OF SILENCE   Organ Dismissal

37
In the Covenant

SACRED ORGAN MUSIC   "Bridegroom of Our Soul"   Drese
CALL TO WORSHIP
HYMN   "O Worship the King"   Attr. Haydn
WORDS OF WELCOME
CALL TO PRAYER   Organ
PASTORAL PRAYER
HYMN   "Praise the Lord, the King of Glory"   Mozart
OLD TESTAMENT LESSON Exodus 24:7
NEW TESTAMENT LESSON   1 Corinthians 11:25
THE MORNING OFFERING
  Duet   The King of Love My Shepherd Is"   Shelley
  Doxology
  Prayer of Dedication

SERMON   "The Lord's Presence—In the Covenant"

"Then he took the book of the covenant, and read it in the hearing of the people; and they said, 'All that the Lord has spoken we will do, and we will be obedient' " (Ex. 24:7).

"Behold the days are coming, says the Lord, when I will make a new covenant with the house of Israel and the house of Judah ... I will put my law within them, and I will write it upon their heart; and I will be their God, and they shall be my people ... I will forgive their iniquity, and I will remember their sin no more (Jer. 31:31-34).

"This cup is the new covenant in my blood [at the cost of His blood]" (1 Cor. 11:25).

Those were dark days indeed when Jeremiah was the prophet of God in Judah. It may be easy to preach when all is going well and the preacher feels successful. But the nation was tottering. The cream of the population was carried away—captives in a foreign Exile. Oh, the bitterness of Exile! The foundations of faith were shaken. The Jewish nation ceased to exist as a political entity. Was there any word from the Lord?

The weeping prophet Jeremiah sounded the bright note of hope in their darkest hour. He promised that God would one day make a new covenant with His people.

In the past, Jehovah had been a covenant-making God. The covenant was one of the great biblical motifs. It appears 286 times from Genesis 17 to Revelation 21. There were several covenant agreements between God and humans. Abraham was chosen by God to become the father of the nation and a man of Faith. He left his home in Ur to follow the Lord's leading—he knew not where. God promised to bless Abraham and make him a blessing to many. His descendants would become a nation. Through Abraham's descendant, the Messiah, all people have been blessed.

At Sinai, God made a covenant with the Israelites. He promised to weld these slaves into a nation and be their God. He gave them His Law, the Ten Commandments, and they promised to be obedient. The covenant was sealed by eating a meal. Moses and his elders "ate and drank" before the Lord (Ex. 24:11). But in time Israel was disobedient, and they went into Exile as a result.

In the future, God promised to make a new covenant with His people. This passage in Jeremiah's prophecy is a high point of Old Testament theology. It gave the name to the great division of the Scriptures: the Old Covenant or testament and the New Covenant or testament.

Jeremiah promised that the New Covenant would be personal. The Old Covenant was corporate—it was made with the nation. The New Covenant would be made with individuals on the basis of faith, not blood lines.

Notice the promises of the New Covenant:

- "I will make a new covenant" (v. 31). It comes by divine initiative, and it will be accomplished by divine power. Where human beings fail, God will achieve.

• "I will put my law within them . . . write it upon their hearts" (v. 33). The Old Covenant was external, written on tablets of stone. The New Covenant will be internal, the law of God within us. God's will and our own wills become identical.

• "I will forgive their iniquity, and I will remember their sin no more" (v. 34). We need divine forgiveness. Notice that God is a good "forgetter."

• "I will be their God, and they shall be my people" (v. 33). Imagine! We can live in a personal faith relationship with our Maker.

The promises of Jeremiah concerning the New Covenant were fulfilled with the coming of the Christ. The kingdom of God became a reality on earth. Those promises are being realized today. To as many as receive Him, He gives power to become the children of God (John 1:12). At the last day, the Kingdom will come completely.

The *sign* of the New Covenant is the Lord's Supper. This cup is the New Covenant at the cost of His life's blood, as Jesus said. The loaf and cup stand for His body and blood sacrifice on the cross for our salvation. Thus, the Lord's Supper is a mighty symbol of our personal relationship with God—in the New Covenant.

Let us examine ourselves, confess our sins, and partake of the Lord's Supper. He is present with us in the New Covenant relationship.

OBSERVANCE OF THE LORD'S SUPPER
  Giving of the Bread
    Chorale   "King of Glory"   J. S. Bach
                         Choir
  Giving of the Cup
    Anthem   "My Eternal King"   Marshall
                         Choir
HYMN   "Fairest Lord Jesus"   arr. Willis
SHARING OF DECISIONS   Benediction
MOMENT OF SILENCE   Organ Dismissal

38
And Power

PRELUDE

HYMN   "Amazing Grace, How Sweet the Sound"
                                fr. *Virginia Harmony*

WELCOME AND PRAYER

HYMN   "Alas, and Did My Savior Bleed"   Wilson

ANTHEM   "Rise Up, O Men of God"   Reed
                        Choir

SERMON   "The Lord's Presence—And Power"

When we open and read the New Testament we are struck with its note of joy and victory. Even as it relates the darkest realities of man's sin and Christ's death, it holds out hope and anticipates ultimate triumph. New Testament people are not left wringing their hands in despair. They are much more apt to be clapping them in praise. They are not cringing and apologetic but bold and confident. They are a real contrast to the attitude of many Christians today. The men and women of the early church appear as persons magnificently alive, and most often hilariously happy. After all, the word which Jesus applied to Kingdom persons in the Beatitudes was *mikarios*—"blessed," O how happy, to be congratulated!

The New Testament church was a singing, victorious church which conquered the paganism of the Roman world. They had a deep assurance of God's presence, His purpose for creation, and His ultimate victory over evil. They were convinced that God was active in their

144

time and in their lives. They were endued with the power of the Holy
Spirit to witness to this exciting faith.

The triumphant New Testament church is a contrast to our modern
preoccupation with problems. We need an antidote for our negative
syndrome. All we seem to talk about is what's wrong with the government, schools, business, the church, youth, or "the establishment." It
doesn't take a lot of brains to be a critic. It does take brain power,
energy, and dedicated hard work to make things different and right
in our world.

The Lord's Table is a place to remember that we don't have to keep
step with the world to be happy. We can march to the sound of a
Different Drummer. God has come into His world in the person of
His Son, Jesus Christ, and the world can never be the same again. This
is the Christmas message. Christ who was brutally killed has been
raised from the dead by the power of God—and is alive, here, today.
That is the good news of the Easter message. Thus, we find comfort,
encouragement, and faith in the celebration of the Lord's Supper. It
serves as a recurring reminder that our God is able.

Christ Is Able to Save Completely

Saul was trusting in good works to save him, including stamping
out the early Christian church. But God saved Saul by grace, and he
became the missionary apostle to the Gentiles.

Slave trader John Newton was a man enslaved by sin, and Christ
liberated him. He became a free man and follower of Christ till his
death.

Many believers today can testify, "My life was rootless, lacking any
sense of direction. Christ saved me and got me off the meaningless
treadmill. He gave me a purpose for living."

Someone else will testify, "I was worried and guilt-ridden. I lived
in fear, despising myself and others. Christ forgave my sins, showed
me that I had worth, and gave me peace."

Faith in Christ results in sins forgiven and lives transformed.
Countless believers have found that God is able to save in every way.
The Supper celebrates that salvation.

Christ Is Able to Help Those Who Are Tempted (Hebrews 2:18)

Peter was troubled by his temper, and Thomas found the resurrection hard to believe. All men, ancient and modern, have known the temptations of the sins of the flesh. Which of us has not done something stupid which we later regretted? Even more subtle are the sins of the spirit such as pride, greed, and hatred. Who is exempt from such temptations and sins?

Christ understands the drag of temptation. He, too, was tempted and resisted the tempter's attractions. Therefore, He understands what we face and can help us answer no to Satan. Remember that with every temptation, God provides a way out (see 1 Cor. 10:13). He is able and will make us strong to resist the evil and do the right.

Christ Is Able to Keep Us from Falling

"Now unto him that is able to keep you from falling, and to present you faultless before the presence of his glory with exceeding joy" (Jude 24, KJV).

James Stewart reminded us that our faith is not simply an ambulance on the battlefield there to deal with casualties. It is itself the armor which protects us. It is not merely a cure for a disease, it is more like preventative medicine which keeps us well.[23]

The Lord's Supper is participation in the body and blood of Christ which helps to keep us spiritually strong. Our worship gives His preventive grace an opportunity to equip us for tough times. I had a friend who lost his son in the war. Once I asked him how he was able to bear it. "Oh," he replied, "the Lord got me ready for that long before it came." Trouble can make us bitter, or it can strengthen our faith and make us stronger. Our attitudes can determine which way we react. Let us trust Him day by day. Our God is able. Indeed, "He is able to do infinitely more than we ask or imagine" (Eph. 3:20). We may trust him completely.

Let us approach the Lord's table in faith and confidence. For our God is able, and He is a present help.

OBSERVANCE OF THE LORD'S SUPPER
  Giving of the Bread
    Solo   "Just Because You Asked"   Harris
  Giving of the Cup
                        "In Remembrance"   Red
                            Choir
CHORAL BENEDICTION
"Go Forth into the World in Peace"   Sjolund
                    Choir and Violin

39
The Holy Spirit

SACRED ORGAN MUSIC
          "From Heaven Above to Earth I Come"   Bohm
CHIMING OF THE HOUR
INVOCATION
HYMN OF PRAISE   "Come, Thou Almighty King"   Giardini
WELCOME TO OUR GUESTS
SOLO   "Trust in Him"   Hamblen
SCRIPTURE READING   John 16:4-15
CALL TO PRAYER
PASTORAL PRAYER
HYMN OF THE HOLY SPIRIT   American Psalm Tune
          "Come, Holy Spirit, Heavenly Dove"
THE MORNING OFFERING
ANTHEM   "Behold Now, Praise the Lord"   Titcomb
Behold now, praise the Lord, all ye servants of the Lord.
Ye that by night stand in the house of the Lord, even in the courts
of the house of our God, lift up your hands in the sanctuary and praise
the Lord.

Gloria Patri   First Setting
Prayer of Dedication
A UNISON READING   "We Believe"
We believe in God the Father Almighty, Maker of heaven and earth;
and in Jesus Christ, His only Son, our Lord,
Who was conceived of the Holy Spirit,
Born of the Virgin Mary,
Suffered under Pontius Pilate, was crucified, dead and buried;
Who was raised from the dead on the third day,
And Who is coming again to judge the living and the dead.
We believe in the Holy Spirit,
The Church as the body of Christ,
The forgiveness of sins, the resurrection of the dead, and life eternal.

SERMON   "The Lord's Presence—The Holy Spirit"

What is the gospel? The gospel is:
The life of Christ—we are saved by His life.
The death of Christ—we are saved by His death on the cross.
The resurrection of Christ—we are living on the right side of Easter!
The gospel is the gift of the Holy Spirit.
In John 16, Jesus promised the gift of the Holy Spirit. There He
described the Spirit's work out in the world and within the church.
In the upper room, Jesus "breathed" on His disciples and said,
"Receive the Holy Spirit" (John 20:22).
At the harvest feast of Pentecost, all the believers were gathered in
one place. There was a noise like strong wind that filled the place.
Each worshiper was touched with a tongue of fire and filled with the
Holy Spirit.

The Holy Spirit and the World Without (John 16:8-11)

1. The Holy Spirit does an exposé of the world. He exposes its
standards of morality and its conclusions about Jesus. The Holy Spirit
is our Advocate and Counselor. These are words which describe a

prosecuting attorney. He takes the stand against the world, convicting it. He shows the world up for what it is.

The Spirit convicts the world of sin. He shows that unbelief is the sin most epitomizing. The authorities had Jesus crucified. They thought they were doing this in the service of God. They considered Him a "criminal" who was leading a rebellion against Rome, a "heretic" who claimed to be the Son of God. They thought Jesus was guilty and that they were right.

What changed their attitude and showed them that they were wrong? It was The Holy Spirit who convicted them of sin. On the day of Pentecost, these very men were pricked in their consciences.

2. The Spirit convinces the world that Jesus Christ was right. The cross appeared to be defeat, but the resurrection was sheer victory. What made mankind see this? The Holy Spirit. The Roman centurion cried, "Truly this man was the Son of God!" (Mark 15:39). Saul, the persecutor of the church, was stopped in his tracks and turned around at his conversion. He was convinced by the Holy Spirit that Jesus Christ was who He claimed to be.

3. The Spirit calls the world into judgment. Judgment is not just some far-off cosmic event. It occurs the moment a person confronts Christ. Judgment occurs here and now, as well as hereafter.

An American tourist was viewing some Renaissance art but was unimpressed. The guide chided him, "Sir, these paintings are not on trial; you are."

The Holy Spirit and Believers (John 16:12-15)

Jesus told His disciples that He was going away, and they would grieve (v. 20, NEB). They were filled with sorrow. How very human! We have sorrow at the loss of a loved one, even when we know they go to a far better world. But Christians do not have to "sorrow as others do who have no hope" (1 Thess. 4:13).

Jesus advised His disciples, "It is to your advantage that I go away" (v. 7). They could not see that, but it was true. We say, "If only I could have seen Christ and known Him in person." Think of it—what if He were still bodily on earth? His presence would be so local and limited that it would be a tragedy rather than a blessing. Jesus ascended to the Father and the Holy Spirit came. This was far better both for them and us.

1. The Spirit will "guide you into all the truth" (v. 13). Consider the confusion in today's world. Note the world's standards and philosophies. The educator is caught up in the conflicting philosophies of education. The businessman or businesswoman lives in a world filled with greed and lacking ethics. The statesman confronts self-interest, war, and suspicion.

The Holy Spirit applies the teachings of Jesus and biblical principles to our everyday life situations. Thus, we live on a pilgrimage of discovery with Him as our Guide.

The Holy Spirit reveals the truth not only to theologians and preachers, but He gives impetus to the Christian poet, the musician, and the scientist who make discoveries.

The surgeon who learns a new procedure to ease the pain of his patient or to spare the patient's life surely is led by the Lord. All truth is God's truth; therefore, we need never fear the truth. Truth is not human discovery so much as God's gift. Truth comes not only from a creed or The Book but also from a Person. Our God is inexhaustible. There are no limits to His love, His knowledge, and His truth. His Holy Spirit is anxious to reveal them to us.

2. The Holy Spirit saves us from every fad that comes along. He keeps the church from being victimized by the tyranny of the temporary. He saves us from falling into the trap of "neology"—the worship of the new and fashionable. The saddest conformist is the one who is conformed to the world and its changing standards. The Scripture admonishes us not to be conformed to this world but to be transformed by the renewing of our minds from within (see Rom. 12:2).

Let the Holy Spirit change you. He wants to be your source of help. He is the very Presence of God.

HYMN OF INVITATION "Breathe on Me, Breath of God" Jackson
SHARING OF DECISIONS   Concerns of the Church
BENEDICTION   Choral Amen
ORGAN DISMISSAL

40
Through Open Doors

HANDBELL PRELUDE
OPENING SENTENCES
HYMN OF COMMITMENT   "Lead On, O King Eternal"   Smart
WORDS OF WELCOME AND CONGREGATIONAL CONCERNS
SCRIPTURE READING
CALL TO PRAYER   "Jesus, Thou Joy of Loving Hearts"   Baker
                                    Choir
PASTORAL PRAYER
THE MORNING OFFERING
  Handbell Offertory
  Gloria Patri
  Prayer of Dedication
HYMN OF DISCIPLESHIP "The Master Hath Come" Welsh Melody

SERMON "The Lord's Presence—Through Open Doors"

"I am the door; if any one enters by me, he will be saved, and will
go in and out and find pasture" (John 10:9)

In ancient times, the sheepfold would be an enclosure of rock or
thorn bushes. There was no door as such but an opening through
which the sheep entered. At night the shepherd might sit in the
opening and literally become the door, protecting those in his charge
from harm.

Jesus said we enter the Kingdom by Him. We are saved by faith

151

in Christ. Paul sounded a similar note when he wrote "through him we both have access in one Spirit to the Father" (Eph. 2:18).

The Master said we "go in and out." Our salvation is not static but dynamic. He does not mean we are saved and lost again. Rather the image is of one on pilgrimage. We come in to worship, go out to serve without fear, but with peace and safety. The reason for our security is that Jesus is the Good Shepherd.

In the Apocalypse, the risen Christ spoke of other doors:

The Door of Relationship

"Behold, I stand at the door and knock; if any one hears my voice and opens the door, I will come in to him and eat with him, and he with me" (Rev. 3:20). This is the door of the human heart. By faith we give Christ access to ourselves and our loyalty.

There is beautiful imagery here: the seeking Christ in quest of souls. This understanding of God is unique to the Christian faith. God seeks people; he takes the initiative in our salvation. This text is an invitation to live in a personal relationship with the Christ. He speaks of our having table fellowship with Him.

In Christ's day breakfast was simple. Lunch was also a light meal eaten during a midday pause in the workday. The main meal of the day was supper. It was eaten in the intimacy of the family and was a time of lingering fellowship. Jesus wants to sup with us—to share fellowship at our supper table. Obviously, the Lord's Supper is a symbol of a fellowship meal. Imagine being at table in the Presence of the Risen Christ!

It is our responsibility to open the door and invite Christ into our lives. He will not force His way. You may recall the famous painting in Saint Paul's Cathedral in London. It shows the Lord Christ standing, knocking at the heart's door. Someone noticed that there is no latch on the door. The artist explained that it is on the inside! Christ knocks, but we must open the door and invite Him in.

The Door of Opportunity

"Behold, I have set before you an open door, which no one is able to shut" (Rev. 3:8). Opportunity is the gift of God. He opens the door.

The apostle Paul wrote about the opportunity in missions using this metaphor, "A great and effectual door is opened unto me" (1 Cor. 16:9, KJV).

All Christians have opportunities to witness to their faith. Look for the open door. Be sensitive to those with whom you can speak a word for Christ. The result of such witness is the Master's approval—and more opportunities to make His presence known.

The Door of Heaven

"I looked, and lo, in heaven an open door!" (Rev. 4:1). In glory we will enter the very presence of God. And we will be reunited with those who have gone on before us. Boundless joy awaits.

The Lord's Supper is a "foretaste of glory divine!"

OBSERVANCE OF THE LORD'S SUPPER
Giving of the Bread
Duet   "Beneath the Cross of Jesus"   arr. Schmidt
Giving of the Cup
Anthem   "Speak to My Heart"   arr. Angell
HYMN OF INVITATION
"Where He Leads Me"   Norris
FELLOWSHIP OFFERING
SHARING OF DECISIONS   Benediction
MOMENT OF SILENCE   Organ Dismissal

Notes

1. Words by Maltbie D. Babcock, "This Is My Father's World.

2. Words by John Bakewell, "Hail, Thou Once Despised Jesus."

3. Words by Lucy Larcom, "Draw Thou My Soul, O Christ"

4. Author Unknown.

5. From *Masterpieces of Religious Verse,* edited by James Dalton Morrison (New York: Harper & Row, 1948), p. 61.

6. William J. Reynolds © 1971 Broadman Press. All rights reserved. Used by permission.

7. Words by Fred Pratt Greer, © 1969 by Hope Publishing Company, Carol Stream, IL. All rights reserved. Used by permission.

8. From Ps. 40:5; 48:9; 63:3-4.

9. Words by William Whiting, Music by Dykes.

10. Marc Connelly, *The Green Pastures* (New York: Holt, Rinehart, and Winston, 1958), p. 69.

11. E. Lee Phillips, *Prayers for Worship* (Grand Rapids, MI: Baker Book House, 1979), p. 117. Used by permission.

12. R. Leonard Small, *No Uncertain Sound* (Edinburgh: T & T Clark, 1963), p. 45.

13. William Temple, *Readings in St. John* (New York: Macmillan and Company, 1952).

14. Used by permission of Carl Fischer, Inc., New York, New York.

15. Albert Schweitzer, *Quest of the Historical Jesus* (New York: Macmillan and Company, 1961), p. 401.

16. Words, William L. Hendricks, 1974. © Copyright 1975 Broadman Press. All rights reserved. Used by permission.

17. Phillips, Ibid., p. 42.

18. E. Glenn Hinson, *The Reaffirmation of Prayer* (Nashville: Broadman Press, 1979), p. 84.

19. G. T. Sparkman, *Writing Your Own Worship Materials* (Valley Forge: PA: Judson Press, 1980), pp. 20-21.

20. Words, Samuel Crossman, 1664.

21. Phillips, Ibid., p. 115.

22. Elton Trueblood, *Foundations for Reconstruction* (New York: Harper & Brothers, 1946), p. 106.

23. James Stewart, *The Wind of the Spirit* (London: Hodder & Stoughton, 1968), pp. 258*ff.*